QUIZZING
ON
BANKING AND FINANCE

QUIZZING ON BANKING AND FINANCE

Gautam Majumdar
Banking and Finance Consultant

Himalaya Publishing House
MUMBAI • NEW DELHI • NAGPUR • BENGALURU • HYDERABAD • CHENNAI • PUNE
LUCKNOW • AHMEDABAD • ERNAKULAM • BHUBANESWAR • INDORE • KOLKATA • GUWAHATI

First Edition : 2013

Published by : Mrs. Meena Pandey for **Himalaya Publishing House Pvt. Ltd.**,
"Ramdoot", Dr. Bhalerao Marg, Girgaon, **Mumbai - 400 004.**
Phone: 022-23860170/23863863, Fax: 022-23877178
E-mail: himpub@vsnl.com; Website: www.himpub.com

Branch Offices :

New Delhi : "Pooja Apartments", 4-B, Murari Lal Street, Ansari Road, Darya Ganj, New Delhi - 110 002. Phone: 011-23270392, 23278631; Fax: 011-23256286

Nagpur : Kundanlal Chandak Industrial Estate, Ghat Road, Nagpur - 440 018. Phone: 0712-2738731, 3296733; Telefax: 0712-2721215

Bengaluru : No. 16/1 (Old 12/1), 1st Floor, Next to Hotel Highlands, Madhava Nagar, Race Course Road, Bengaluru - 560 001. Phone: 080-32919385; Telefax: 080-22286611

Hyderabad : No. 3-4-184, Lingampally, Besides Raghavendra Swamy Matham, Kachiguda, Hyderabad - 500 027. Phone: 040-27560041, 27550139; Mobile: 09390905282

Chennai : No. 8/2, Modley 2nd Street, Ground Floor, T. Nagar, Chennai - 600 017. Phone: 044-28144004/28144005; Mobile: 09345345051

Pune : First Floor, "Laksha" Apartment, No. 527, Mehunpura, Shaniwarpeth (Near Prabhat Theatre), Pune - 411 030. Phone: 020-24496323/24496333; Mobile: 09370579333

Lucknow : House No. 731, Sehkhupura Colony, Near B.D. Convent School, Lucknow -226024. Mobile : 09307501549

Ahmedabad : 114, "SHAIL", 1st Floor, Opp. Madhu Sudan House, C.G. Road, Navrang Pura, Ahmedabad - 380 009. Phone: 079-26560126; Mobile: 09377088847

Ernakulam : 39/104 A, Lakshmi Apartment, Karikkamuri Cross Rd., Ernakulam, Cochin - 622011, Kerala. Phone: 0484-2378012, 2378016; Mobile: 09344199799

Bhubaneswar : 5 Station Square, Bhubaneswar - 751 001 (Odisha). Phone: 0674-2532129, Mobile: 09338746007

Indore : Kesardeep Avenue Extension, 73, Narayan Bagh, Flat No. 302, IIIrd Floor, Near Humpty Dumpty School, Indore - 452 007 (M.P.). Mobile: 09301386468

Kolkata : 108/4, Beliaghata Main Road, Near ID Hospital, Opp. SBI Bank, Kolkata - 700 010, Phone: 033-32449649, Mobile: 09910440956

Guwahati : House No. 15, Behind Pragjyotish College, Near Sharma Printing Press, P.O. Bharalumukh, Guwahati - 781009, (Assam). Mobile: 09883055590, 09883055536

Typeset at : Elite-Art, New Delhi
Printed at : Krishna Offset Press, Delhi

Preface

Quizzing is an intellectual exercise which is extremely stimulating. It kindles interest in different subjects for increasing the knowledge base and stokes the passion of an individual for honing and demonstrating his abilities. There is the competitive flavour in quizzing which is essentially a mind game. Many others look at it as a pastime, well spent.

Whichever way it is seen, there is no doubt that quiz competitions generate tremendous interest among people. There is feverish activity among the participants to excel as success in quiz contests tends to elevate the intellectual status of an individual. It certainly brings a sense of superiority as it bestows pride and confidence for being knowledgeable. Competitions are an effective way of popularizing subjects, themes among homogeneous group of people. Quiz competitions have therefore become fairly popular with all groups at different levels to promote the intended message.

Be it school or college going students, the office executives, business school students, there are quiz competitions engaging each of these groups. Business and finance being an area which impacts all, it is increasingly visible that many quiz contests are being modelled on this functional topic.

This book has been written primarily to enlarge the area of interest in banking, business, finance and money and to present a large canvas of issues from this area in the form of thought-provoking questions. The methodology employed is the direct question answer and the multiple options format. Certain issues would find mention at more than one place in alternative ways in order that the different dimensions of the subject are presented. Chapterization has been done with focus on different segments of the vast financial sector to expose the reader to the enormous range each segment covers. The interest is sought to be sustained by learning about the evolution of the different strands of finance, the growth and sophistication of each branch, the famous and not so famous personalities who have contributed to these areas, the institutions which have formalized the working and the practices, products and services which have taken shape in this continuing journey.

The author is confident that the curiosity quotient of the reader would be activated and satiated after going through the contents of the book. It should make for an interesting and absorbing reading as the questions have been presented after painstaking research. A fairly voluminous collection of questions, rich in content, some reasonably simple and some not so, would certainly test the intelligence quotient of the reader.

HAPPY QUIZZING!

— Gautam Majumdar

Contents

QUIZ ONE

Financial History – India

Q. Which were the first coins of India?

A. Silver punch marked coins.

Q. Which Act permitted the production of paper currency in India?

A. The Paper Currency Act, 1861.

Q. Which Act in India is relevant for the production of coins?

A. The Indian Coinage Act.

Q. When did the decimal system start in India?

A. 1957.

Q. What were the units of coins before the start of the decimal system in India?

A. Anna, pie, and pice.

Q. When did India introduce its first paper money?

A. In 1861, 10 rupee notes were introduced.

Q. When was the first commemorative coin issued in India?

A. In 1964.

Q. How many 'annas' were equal to a rupee?

A. 16 annas made one rupee.

Q. What was the smallest denomination of coin during the period of 'annas'?

A. pie.

Q. Which banking institutions are considered to have started banking in India towards the end of the eighteenth century?

A. General Bank of India (1786) and The Bank of Hindusthan (1790).

Q. The sculptures of Yaksha and Yakshini flank the entrance of the New Delhi office of the Reserve Bank of India. Which Indian artist executed their sculptures?

A. Ram Kinkar Baij.

Q. Which Asian nation was the first to get a World Bank loan for development projects?

A. India in 1944 for railway reconstruction and development.

Q. What was the currency of India during British rule?

A. The rupee was the currency which was a silver coin of 91.7% silver by weight at 11.60 grams.

Q. When was the one rupee currency note first introduced?

A. In 1914.

Q. Who was the signatory on the one rupee currency notes?

A. Finance Secretary, Government of India.

Q. Production of one rupee notes has since been discontinued. When did it stop?

A. 1994.

Q. Which authority is vested with the power to mint coins in India?

A. Government of India.

Q. Who is responsible for the production of currency notes in India?

A. Reserve Bank of India.

Q. What is the maximum denomination of currency notes that can be printed in India?

A. ₹ 10,000.

Q. Which are the security features of a currency note in India?

A. Security thread, intaglio printing, water mark, etc.

Q. What is the origin of the word 'rupee'?

A. The word 'rupee' is derived from the Sanskrit word 'rupyakani'.

Q. In how many languages does the word 'rupee' appear on the currency notes?

A. 15.

Q. What is the maximum denomination for which coins can be produced in India?

A. ₹ 1,000.

Q. Which is the minimum denomination of coin that is accepted as legal tender in India?

A. 50 paise coins.

Q. When was the Indian rupee given a symbol?

A. 2010.

Q. Which person is credited with designing the symbol for the Indian rupee?

A. D. Udaya Kumar.

Q. Which other currencies of the world have a distinctive symbol?

A. US $, pound sterling, Japanese Yen, Euro.

Q. How was the design for the Indian rupee selected?

A. Through an open competition held by the Government of India.

Q. What is the name given to the rental value of borrowed money?

A. Interest.

Q. Which state in India during British rule had its own currency?

A. Hyderabad.

Q. Which is the oldest stock exchange in India?

A. Bombay Stock Exchange – BSE.

Q. Which denomination of the rupee was the first to be introduced?

A. In 1861 it was the 10 rupee notes that were first introduced.

Q. When did RBI begin note production?

A. In 1938.

Q. The Banking Companies (Transfer and Acquisition of Undertaking) Act, 1970 and 1980 are applicable to which banks?

A. Nationalized banks.

Q. RBI can issue notes up to what denomination?

A. ₹ 10,000.

Q. Before nationalization of the Reserve Bank of India what was its status?

A. It was a private shareholders' institution.

Q. The history of Reserve Bank of India mentions that the share issue of the bank offered at that time was the biggest in India. When was the share issue of RBI offered?

A. In 1935.

Q. Reserve Bank of India began its operations by taking over from the Imperial Bank of India the management of government accounts and public debt and from the government the functions performed by a particular department. Which was this particular department?

A. The Controller of Currency.

Q. Which was the first Indian bank to be wholly-owned and managed by Indians?

A. Central Bank of India in 1911.

Q. After partition Reserve Bank of India served as the Central Bank of Pakistan till a particular period. Till which date did RBI perform this responsibility?

A. Till June 1948.

Q. Which institution took over as the Central Bank of Pakistan from the Reserve Bank of India in 1948?

A. State Bank of Pakistan.

Q. Which State/UT of India was declared as the first among these geographical regions to achieve the milestone of cent per cent coverage of all villages under the financial inclusion programme?

A. Union Territory of Pondicherry.

Q. Reserve Bank of India served as the central bank of yet another neighbouring country twice till April 1947. Which was this country?

A. Burma now Myanmar.

Q. The word 'Rupiya' was coined by Sher Shah Suri during his reign from 1540-1545. What physical form did it represent?

A. 'Rupiya' was a silver coin weighing roughly 11.54 grams.

Q. Taken from Kautilya's Arthashashtra which body of the Indian Government has these Sanskrit words 'Kosha Moolo Dandaha' as its motto?

A. The Income Tax department.

Q. Which public sector bank had its headquarters inaugurated by Mahatma Gandhi?

A. Union Bank of India.

Q. This body which is a part of the RBI was constituted in 1994 to undertake integrated supervision of banks, non-banking financial companies and financial institutions. Which is this authority?

A. Board for Financial Supervision – BFS.

Q. In the Indian economic context which significant reform was introduced by the government in 1957?

A. The introduction of the decimal coinage system.

Q. An important constitutional authority is responsible for establishing and maintaining a sound and efficient accounting and financial audit reporting system in India. Which is this authority?

A. The Comptroller and Auditor General CAG.

Q. In order to ensure the safety of deposits of small depositors in banks in India an important legislation was passed. Which was this law that was enacted in 1961?

A. The Deposit Insurance Corporation Act, 1961.

Q. When was State Bank of India constituted?

A. 1st July, 1955.

Q. When was the State Bank of India Act passed by the Parliament?

A. In 1955.

Q. How many associate banks were taken over by State Bank of India and when?

A. 8 associate banks in 1959.

Q. How did State Bank of Bikaner and Jaipur come into being?

A. State Bank of Bikaner and State Bank of Jaipur merged in 1963 to become the State Bank of Bikaner and Jaipur.

Q. Before becoming associate banks of State Bank of India what were these banks known as?

A. These were banks of the respective Princely States of India.

Q. Which bank came into existence in 1921 when three banks, *viz.*, Bank of Bengal (1806), Bank of Bombay (1840) and Bank of Madras (1843) were reorganized and amalgamated to form a single banking organization?

A. Imperial Bank of India.

Q. When did the government pass the State Bank (Subsidiary Bank) Act?

A. In 1959.

Q. The bank which was the first to be established by Indian merchants completed 100 years of its existence recently. Name this bank?

A. Central Bank of India.

Q. Which was the first commercial bank of India in the history of banking industry in India?

A. Hindustan Bank.

Q. What was the criteria for the second round of nationalization of six banks in India in 1980?

A. Private banks which had deposits of ₹ 200 crore and above were nationalized.

Q. Name the bank which was the first to introduce a pygmy savings scheme under which small amounts as low as 25 paise were collected daily from the depositor's residence?

A. Syndicate Bank.

Q. Which was the first public sector bank to introduce the ATM in India?

A. Bank of Baroda.

Q. Which bank was conducting transactions on behalf of the British government till 1935?

A. Imperial Bank of India.

Q. By what name did Imperial Bank of India later came to be known as?

A. State Bank of India.

Q. Which of the public sector banks in India is the oldest?

A. Allahabad Bank.

Q. Which is the Indian bank which started in Lahore and later shifted to India after partition?

A. Punjab National Bank.

Q. What may be regarded as the first formal regulation for the working of banks in India?

A. The enactment of the Companies Act in 1850.

Q. Which popular movement in India was largely responsible for starting a number of commercial banks during the 1920s?

A. The Swadeshi movement.

Q. What is the name of the first regional rural bank in India?

A. Prathama Bank.

Q. When was the Banking Regulation Act enacted in India?

A. In 1949.

Q. Reserve Bank of India was established on the basis of the recommendations of a commission. What was the name of this commission?

A. Hilton Young Commission.

Q. The Hilton Young Commission was known by another official name. What was this name?

A. The Royal Commission on Indian Currency and Finance 1926.

Q. What particular item/symbol/movement was the inspiration for finalizing the emblem for the Reserve Bank of India?

A. East India Company's double mohur.

Q. What does the emblem of Reserve Bank of India depict?

A. A tiger and a palm tree.

Q. Where was Reserve Bank of India's first central office located?

A. Calcutta.

Q. When did Reserve Bank of India celebrate its platinum jubilee?

A. During 2009-10.

Q. What was the initial share capital of Reserve Bank of India when it started?

A. ₹ 5 crore.

Q. Who was the first Indian Governor of Reserve Bank of India?

A. C D Deshmukh.

Q. Who was the first Governor of Reserve Bank of India?

A. Sir Osborne Smith in 1935.

Q. Paper money was first introduced in which country around 800 AD?

A. China.

Q. Which was the first cooperative bank to be established in India?

A. Anyonya Cooperative Bank.

Q. What was achieved by passing the Banking Companies Act, 1969?

A. Nationalization of 14 commercial banks.

Q. When was the first one paisa coin under the decimal system issued in India?

A. March 1962.

Q. Which was the first public sector mutual fund that was set-up in India after the Unit Trust of India?

A. SBI Mutual Fund.

Q. In which year was Life Insurance Corporation of India created?

A. 1st September, 1956 after Parliament passed the LIC Act in June 1956.

Q. This institution is regarded as the second oldest surviving deposit insurance agency in the world. It was established in 1962. Which is this agency?

A. Deposit Insurance Credit Guarantee Corporation.

Q. The note issuing department of the Reserve Bank of India should always possess the minimum specified amount of gold stock. What is this figure?

A. ₹ 115 crore worth of gold.

Q. Life insurance business in India is more than two hundred years old. What did the Indian Life Assurance Companies Act, 1912 achieve in this regard?

A. It was the first statutory measure to regulate life insurance business.

Q. In 1991, India faced huge balance of payments crisis and had to shore up its reserves. What momentous decision did it take to set right the reserves position?

A. It pledged its gold reserves to borrow foreign exchange.

Q. In 1818, this company was the first life insurer to start business in India. It failed in 1834 and shut shop. Which life insurance company are we talking abcut?

A. Oriental Life Insurance Company.

Q. The first life insurance company in India was started by the Europeans in 1818. Which was the life insurance business that was first established by the Indians?

A. Bombay Mutual Life Assurance Society in 1870.

Q. There is a period in time which was known as the Free Banking Era in India. During this time banks in India were free to issue cheques and promissory notes payable to bearer on demand. Can you identify the time period?

A. It is the time period up to 1861 when the Paper Currency Act, 1861 was enacted.

Q. Banking Companies Act, 1949 was enacted to give the Reserve Bank of India the power to regulate the banking sector in India. It was renamed later in 1966. By what name was the Act later known as?

A. Banking Regulation Act, 1949.

Q. In 1861 the British government of India introduced its first paper money. When did Reserve Bank of India begin printing of currency notes in India?

A. In 1938.

Q. Which well known personality was the first to estimate the national income of India?

A. Dadabhai Naoroji.

Q. Which legislation gave Reserve Bank of India the authority to act as the banker to the Central Government?

A. RBI Act, 1934.

Q. Nationalization of banks was part of the social control that the government had started in India. When was the priority sector lending targets introduced as part of social control?

A. 1974.

Q. Which was the first mutual fund company that was established in India?

A. The Unit Trust of India.

Q. The private sector in India was given permission to enter the mutual fund industry after the start of business by the public sector. Which private sector company was the first to set up a mutual fund company?

A. Kothari Pioneer in 1993.

Q. The symbol for the rupee was finalized from a countrywide design contest. On which script is the symbol based on?

A. Mix of Devanagri and Roman script.

Q. The evolution of money in India has been traced through its coinage and financial instruments. There is a place in Mumbai which show cases this treasure and gives a glimpse into India's financial history. Which is this place that we are talking about?

A. Reserve Bank of India's Monetary Museum.

Q. The earliest documented coins of India are silver punch marked coins. To which particular time period in history were the coins related to?

A. Around 6th century BC.

Q. Which was the date which marked the issue of the coinage of the Indian republic?

A. 15th August, 1950.

Q. As a result of the nationalization of the general insurance business in India, 107 insurers were merged to form new companies. When did this nationalization happen?

A. 1st January, 1973.

Q. Four companies were formed as a result of the merger of the 107 companies of general insurance. Which were these companies apart from National Insurance Co. Ltd?

A. The other three companies were New India Assurance Co. Ltd., Oriental Insurance Co. Ltd., and United India Insurance Co. Ltd.

Q. Which was the committee set-up in 1993 to propose recommendations for reforms in the insurance sector in India?

A. Malhotra Committee.

Q. Insurance Regulatory Development Authority (IRDA) is the regulator for the insurance sector in India. When was this body set-up?

A. In the year 2000.

Q. Sher Shah Suri is acknowledged to have first introduced the copper coin along with the gold mohur and rupiya the silver coin. What was the name of this copper coin?

A. 'dam'.

Q. When one rupee was equivalent to 16 annas, how many rupees equalled one mohur?

A. 15 rupees.

Q. Hundis are the oldest form of credit instruments that were used. To which period can you relate the use of hundis?

A. 12th century AD.

Q. If you were told that the term 'Rnam-Sam-m' was commonly used in ancient India in the context of loans what would you understand?

A. The term meant paying off a debt.

Q. Can you mention the words which were used in earlier times in India to indicate the documents executed for getting loans?

A. 'rnapatra' and 'rnalekhya'.

Q. The Western variety of joint stock banking was brought to India by the English agency houses of Calcutta and Bombay. Which was the first joint stock bank that was set-up in Bombay in 1720?

A. Bank of Bombay.

Q. Which was the first Presidency bank that was established in India with a capital of ₹ 50 lakh?

A. Bank of Bengal in 1806.

Q. The second Presidency bank was set-up in 1840 with a capital of ₹ 52 lakh. Which was this bank?

A. Bank of Bombay.

Q. The Bank of Madras was the third Presidency bank set-up in 1843. What was the starting capital for this bank?

A. ₹ 30 lakh.

Q. Why were the Bank of Bengal, Bank of Bomb y and Bank of Madras known as Presidency banks?

A. They were known as Presidency banks because they we e set-up in the three Presidencies that were units of administrative jurisdictions in the country for the East India Company.

Q. The Imperial Bank of India was established as a result of the amalgamation of the three Presidency banks in 1921. The Imperial Bank was later further re constituted with the merger of a number of other banks. Which were these banks?

A. These banks belonged to the old princely states such as Jaipur, Mysore, Patiala and Jodhpur.

Q. The Imperial Bank of India acted as the central bank prior to the establishment of the Reserve Bank in 1935. It performed two other banking roles as well. Which were these functions?

A. The role of a commercial bank and banker to the government.

Q. For safety of deposits of small depositors in banks in India, the Deposit Insurance Act 1961 was enacted. India was one of the few countries to introduce such deposit insurance. Which was the first country to introduce deposit insurance?

A. USA.

Q. The post office savings bank was started in India to promote small savings scheme. When did this small savings scheme originate?

A. In 1882.

Q. All the small savings scheme are operated through approximately 1,50,000 post offices across the country. There is however one scheme which is also available at designated branches of public sector banks and select private sector banks. Which is this scheme?

A. Public Provident Fund (PPF) scheme.

Q. The small savings schemes are managed by an independent authority under the Ministry of Finance, Government of India. Which is this department?

A. National Small Savings Fund – NSSF.

Q. In order to enable banks to recover their past dues 'The Recovery of Debts due to Banks and Financial Institutions Act' was enacted in 1993. This Act led to the establishment of certain bodies for adjudication and recovery of dues. Which bodies are we talking about?

A. Debt recovery tribunals and debt recovery appellate tribunals were established all across the country.

Q. Reserve Bank of India took a significant step in 1995 for addressing customer grievances in commercial banks. This mechanism was set-up under the provisions of the Banking Regulation Act, 1949. Name the scheme?

A. The Banking Ombudsman scheme.

Q. The shortfalls in priority sector lending of public and private sector banks are meant to be deposited in the Rural Infrastructure Development Fund. Which particular organization manages this fund?

A. National Bank for Agriculture and Rural Development (NABARD).

Q. The Credit Information Act was passed in 2005 to enable credit information companies to collect, process and share credit information on borrowers of banks/financial institutions. Prior to this law the Union Budget of 2000-01 announced the first major step in this direction. What was the decision of the government that was conveyed?

A. The establishment of Credit Information Bureau India Ltd.

Q. The deposit insurance system is based on a flat rate of premium being paid by banks. Which are the banks which are eligible to get the insurance cover under this system?

(*i*) Scheduled commercial banks

(*ii*) Regional rural banks, urban cooperative banks

(*iii*) Public sector and private sector banks

(*iv*) Only (*i*) and (*ii*).

A. (*iv*).

Q. Which was the first associate bank of State Bank of India?

(*i*) State Bank of Patiala

(*ii*) State Bank of Mysore

(*iii*) State Bank of Hyderabad

(*iv*) State Bank of Travancore.

A. (*iii*).

Q. Which nationalized bank was the first to sponsor a regional rural bank in India?

(*i*) Syndicate Bank

(*ii*) Bank of India

(*iii*) Union Bank of India

(*iv*) Central Bank of India.

A. (*i*).

Q. Which was the first development financial institution in India?

(*i*) IDBI Ltd.

(*ii*) IFCI Ltd.

(*iii*) IIBI

(*iv*) NABARD.

A. (*ii*).

Q. Which development financial institution integrated with a bank?

(*i*) IFCI Ltd.

(*ii*) ICICI Ltd.

(*iii*) NHB

(*iv*) IIFCL.

A. (*ii*).

Q. The origin of the State Bank of India which goes back to the early 19th century may be linked to which of the following?

(*i*) Bank of Bengal

(*ii*) Bank of Calcutta

(*iii*) Bank of Madras

(*iv*) Bank of Bombay.

A. (*ii*).

■■■

QUIZ TWO

Financial History – International

Q. Where in Europe were the first bank notes printed?

A. In Sweden.

Q. How many official currencies are there in the world?

A. 182.

Q. What particular official motto of the US appears on their coins and currencies?

A. 'In GOD We Trust'.

Q. When and where was the first paper money invented?

A. Paper money was first invented around 88 AD in China.

Q. Yen is the official currency of Japan. What is its relation with 'SEN'?

A. 'SEN' is 1/100th of a Yen.

Q. Which country launched the plastic notes first?

A. Australia.

Q. When was the first dollar coin issued in the US?

A. In 1782.

Q. When was the dollar officially accepted as the currency of the US?

A. In 1785.

Q. What is the common name of Canada's 1 dollar coin?

A. Loonie.

Q. Income tax is an important revenue resource for any government. When and where was this form of taxation started?

A. In England in 1799.

Q. It was established in 1157 and is regarded as the earliest ancient bank. Which is this bank?

A. The Bank of Venice.

Q. It is widely regarded that modern banking began with them in the 17th century in London. At that time money was held in the form of gold and silver coins and they had excellent strong rooms which made people keep their money with them for a fee. Who are we talking about?

A. Goldsmiths of London who issued receipts for the safe keeping of the money.

Q. The origin of the word 'bank' is linked to a French word for bench which was used by moneylenders to transact their business. What is this French word?

A. 'Banque'.

Q. Can you name the important French bank which has the word 'banque' in its name?

A. BNP or Banque National de Paris.

Q. An international agreement mandated its member countries to declare the par value of its currency in terms of gold or US dollars. Which was this agreement?

A. The articles of agreement of the International Monetary Fund.

Q. This Viennese classical liberal economist in 1883 provided the theory of the origin of money which suggests that the state has no role to play in the supply of money. If society is left alone money will emerge spontaneously out of trade. All that the state has to do is punish fraud. Who is this well known economist who also chaired a committee on the gold standard?

A. Carl Menger.

Q. The onset of life insurance was seen in England in the 16th century. It was an astronomer in 1693 who worked out the first mortality table on the basis of statistical laws of mortality and compound interest. Who was this astronomer?

A. Edmond Halley.

Q. When did Lloyds of London considered to be the most famous insurance company in the world start its business?

A. In 1689 in a coffee house of Edward Lloyd in Tower Street in London.

Q. In 1850 the British established the first general insurance company in Calcutta. Which was this company?

A. Triton Insurance Company Ltd.

Q. The Dutch East India Co., was the first company to issue stock. The company was granted a monopoly over the Asian trade. It was paying an 18 per cent dividend for almost 200 years till it was dissolved in 1800. What was the reason for its closure?

A. The company became bankrupt.

Q. He was a fortune writer who launched a 'hedged fund' in 1949 that bought stocks and sold them short in order to hedge its exposure to the market ups and downs. The name 'hedge fund' is considered to have originated from him. Who was this personality?

A. Alfred Winslow Jones.

Q. All patents issued by the US Patent and Trademark Office from July 1790 to July 1836 were destroyed in a devastating fire in 1839. These patents are known by a particular name. What is this word?

A. X patents.

Q. What significant development took place with the signing of the Maastricht Treaty in 1992?

A. The formation of the European Union.

Q. The House of Rothschild is a huge name in the world of business since the eighteenth century. With which sector have they been associated?

A. Finance and investments.

Q. Which was the first bank in the world to offer an overdraft facility in 1728?

A. Royal Bank of Scotland.

Q. The oldest surviving bank in the world is located in Italy. It was founded in 1472. What is the name of this bank?

A. Banca Monte dei Paschi di Siena.

Q. World Bank was founded in 1945 after the Second World War. Who was its first President?

A. Eugene Mayer

Q. All Nobel prizes are given by the same Nobel committee except the prize in Economics. Which body instituted this prize?

A. Bank of Sweden.

Q. In 1914 which company offered the first charge card to its customers which were later to become the forerunners of the current day credit cards?

A. Western Union.

Q. These objects found in the shallow waters of the Pacific and Indian oceans were first used as money in China. Which is the object being referred to?

A. Cowrie shells.

Q. In the year 1854 six private banking companies of Basel, Switzerland got together to form the Bankverein, a consortium which acted as an underwriting syndicate for its member banks. What ultimately developed from this association?

A. UBS commonly known as the Swiss Bank.

Q. Which central bank is bestowed with the honour as being the oldest in the world?

A. Bank of Sweden.

Q. The Basel Accord which was signed in 1988 was a landmark in the banking business across the world. What was the purpose of this Accord?

A. It was concerning capital regulation and was designed to establish minimum levels of capital for banks.

Q. Which were the countries that came forward to sign this Basel agreement?

A. 12 countries comprising all G 10 countries plus Luxembourg and Switzerland.

Q. When were Basel I norms introduced for the scheduled commercial banks?

A. In 1992.

Q. The crises in 1982 led to a massive strain on the capital of most banks and triggered the need to formulate regulations in the form of Basel I norms. Which were these events?

A. The Latin American debt crises.

Q. Which international authority is credited with making efforts for creating convergence of supervisory regulations for finalizing the Basel Accord?

A. Basel Committee on Banking Supervision.

Q. Over the years several countries have switched to the risk based deposit insurance system from the fixed premium method. Which country was the first to adopt this method and when?

A. In 1995 only US had the risk based deposit insurance system.

Q. It was an international agreement meant to reduce restrictions in trade between countries. It was replaced in 1995 by a better mechanism in the form of World Trade Organization. Which was the agreement that was replaced?

A. General Agreement on Trade and Tariffs (GATT)

Q. It is a British company that facilitates the trading of European currency. It provides same day transfer for pound sterling and the euro currency. Established in 1984 it eliminates the float time that occurs with cheque payments. Which is this organization?

A. Clearing House Automated Payments System (CHAPS)

Q. CHIPS is a computerized bank clearing system used in the US. What is its full form?

A. Clearing House Inter Bank Payments System.

Q. It is the bank responsible for the monetary system of the European Union and the euro. The bank was founded in Germany in 1998. Which is this bank?

A. European Central Bank.

Q. Marine insurance in its modern concept was introduced by the British with the establishment of the first company in Kolkata in 1710. Which was this company?

A. Sun Insurance Office Ltd.

Q. It is considered as the oldest private bank in Germany which was established in 1590 by Dutch brothers. The bank is still owned by the same dynasty. Can you identify the bank?

A. The Berenberg Bank.

Q. In ancient times the Christians denounced the payment of interest on savings/investments as practice of sin. Which is the word used to describe this practice?

A. Usury.

Q. Which is the currency system which is recognized as the 'Imperial Currency'?

A. The currencies of Pound, Shilling, Pence.

Q. In 1770 this system first started when bank representatives met at the Lombard Street in London to exchange their mutual documents with each other for settlement. What was this activity?

A. It was the start of cheque clearing system amongst banks.

Q. Customers get their personalized cheque books with their names printed on the cheque leaves. In 1811 this particular bank was the first to personalize the customers' cheques by printing the names of the accountholders. Which was this bank?

A. The Commercial Bank of Scotland.

Q. Which bank in 1830 moved a step further in devising a common format by introducing cheque books of 50, 100 and 200 leaves?

A. The Bank of England.

Q. It was the first silver coin which was minted from 1836 to 1839 and struck for circulation in the US after its production was officially halted in 1806. Name this coin?

A. Gobrecht dollar.

Q. Formerly the world's largest company the Dutch East India Company went bankrupt reportedly due to competitive free trade. In which year did it happen?

A. In 1799.

Q. There was much speculation over Greece exiting the European Union owing to its financial crisis. However, which is the only country to have left the European Association so far?

A. Greenland which left the European Economic Community in 1985.

Q. What is the Simpson Bowles effect in the US fiscal negotiations?

A. It was a plan to reduce the Federal deficit by cutting spending and raising taxes which was influencing the fiscal cliff negotiations.

Q. It is considered as the largest bankruptcy filing in US history. The company filed for Chapter 11 bankruptcy in 2008. Which is this company?

A. Lehman Bros Holdings Inc.

Q. US President Abraham Lincoln used these United States notes as legal tender to fund the civil war. These notes also known as Legal Tender notes were a type of paper money issued from 1862 to 1971. What is the special name for these notes?

A. Green backs, a name they derived from the Demand Notes they replaced in 1862.

Q. The US was witnessing numerous runs on banks and the New York Stock Exchange fell almost 50 per cent from its peak the previous year. It was a time of recession and was known as the bankers' panic. What is the term given to indicate this financial crisis in the US?

A. The Panic of 1907.

Q. The Federal Reserve System which was made the central banking authority of the US with the legal authority to issue legal tender was created by which legal Act?

A. The Federal Reserve Act 1913.

Q. The Great Depression was plagued by a series of bank runs which needed to be checked. What particular action is considered to be responsible for putting a stop to the bank runs?

A. The nationwide Bank Holidays from 9th March to 12th March, 1933.

Q. Which US legal provisions are responsible for the establishment of the Federal Deposit Insurance Corporation FDIC in the US in 1933?

A. The Emerging Banking Act of 1933.

Q. Which US President is credited with passing the Emerging Banking Act which allows only Federal Reserve approved banks to operate in the US?

A. Franklin D Roosevelt.

Q. In 1971 the US President Richard Nixon took a series of economic measures which were known as the Nixon shock. What was the critical outcome of these actions?

A. It cancelled the direct convertibility of the US dollar to gold by foreign nations.

Q. This Nixon shock is considered as the economic measure which effectively brought to an end the close of an era brought about by the consequences of World War II. What particular economic aspect was affected and changed?

A. Ended the Bretton Woods system of international financial system of currency exchange.

Q. This unusual phenomenon of using the currency of another country as the *de facto* currency happened in Argentina and Brazil in the 1980s. It was because the people of those countries lost confidence in their own currency as inflation was eroding its value. There is a special term for this phenomenon. Can you name it?

A. Dollarization.

Q. The people of this country were forced to overthrow the country's administration when its economy collapsed in 1997 as a result of the Ponzi schemes. Which was this East European country?

A. Albania.

Q. In 2008 the US saw its largest bank failure in history with the collapse of the largest savings and loan association. Which was this organization?

A. Washington Mutual the owner of Washington Mutual Bank.

Q. We are referring to a global investment bank and securities firm which was based in New York city. In March 2008, JP Morgan Chase had offered to acquire this large financial firm at a price of US$ 2 per share. However, with the sudden turn of events JP Morgan completed its acquisition in May 2008 at a negotiated price of 10 cents per share. Which was this investment bank?

A. Bear Stearns.

Q. The first Basel agreement on global banking regulation adopted in 1988 was 30 pages long and relied on simple arithmetic. The latest update Basel III runs into number of pages and includes 78 calculus equations. Can you indicate the number of pages the report has?

A. 509 pages.

Q. It is widely accepted that cheque as a payment method in addition to a way of transferring funds was first used by this country in the late 1500s. Which country was this?

A. Holland.

Q. Which country is credited with developing the MICR code, which is an integral part of all cheques, in 1959?

A. USA.

Q. The Geneva Convention in 1931 attempted to simplify the laws relating to use of cheques. What was the focus of attention?

A. The unification of laws relating to cheques.

Q. In 1557 this royalty managed to burden his kingdom with so much debt as the result of several pointless wars that he caused the world's first national bankruptcy. It occurred because 40 per cent of the country's GDP was going towards servicing the debt. Identify the royalty of the country which was responsible for it?

A. Phillip II of Spain.

■■■

QUIZ THREE

Money, Finance and Banking-I

Q. What is the meaning of money?

A. It is a medium to facilitate payments.

Q. In what forms is money possible?

A. It is a medium of exchange, unit of account and store of value.

Q. What is understood by the phrase 'time value of money'?

A. The financial aspect which is the interest.

Q. How does the barter system work?

A. The exchange of goods between parties to a deal in the absence of money.

Q. Why was barter system adopted?

A. It was the only method possible to settle transactions when money was not invented.

Q. For something to satisfy the medium of exchange function of money what quality should it possess?

A. Should be readily exchangeable for other goods.

Q. What function of money do you think the price tag on a book represents?

A. The store of value.

Q. What is the name given to the place where coins are produced?

A. Mint.

Q. How is money created in the banking sector?

A. Through printing of currency and creation of loans.

Q. How do banks make money?

A. By giving of loans.

Q. What is meant by the phrase 'there is a run on the bank'?

A. When customers fearing a bank collapse rush to the bank to withdraw their money.

Q. When a person publicly declares his inability to pay what is it known as?

A. Voluntary bankruptcy

Q. How did the US dollar get its name?

A. From the word 'thaler'.

Q. The price of one country's currency in terms of another currency is referred to as?

A. Exchange rate.

Q. What is the impact of inflation on the real value of money?

A. There is difference between the real value and the notional value.

Q. What happens when there is sustained downward movement in the business cycle of an economy?

A. Recession.

Q. What is the name given to the branch of economics which has mathematics and statistics as part of its study?

A. Econometrics.

Q. Which authority controls moneylenders in India?

A. They are unregulated entities.

Q. The government securities on which no interest is paid and only the face value of the bond is paid on maturity are called?

A. Zero coupon bonds.

Q. What is the financial ratio which divides a company's liquid assets by its current liabilities?

A. Current ratio.

Q. Which Central Bank is known as the Old Lady of Threadneedle Street?

A. Bank of England.

Q. Which state in India during British rule had its own currency?

A. Hyderabad.

Q. What is meant by 360 degrees thinking?

A. A term used for considering all options in business as opposed to having narrow field vision.

Q. When banks sell insurance policies what is it called?

A. Bancassurance.

Q. What is understood from the term 'caveat emptor'?

A. Let the buyer beware.

Q. What is the basis of the business of insurance?

A. Uberrima Fides.

Q. What does 'Uberrima Fides' mean?

A. Trust and faith.

Q. Which institution is generally regarded as the first life insurance company in the world?

A. The Amicable Society for a Perpetual Assurance founded in London in 1705.

Q. Known as 'bottomry' it is usually considered as the first insurance activity to initiate the business of insurance as a commercial activity. What was this activity?

A. The insurance of merchant ships' sculls.

Q. In 1694 a group of business men agreed to lend a sum of money to the British government in return for permission to start an institution. This institution is today one of the biggest financial institution in the world. Can you identify this institution?

A. Bank of England.

Q. What was the minimum deposit figure that was necessary for the private commercial banks to be nationalized in 1969 in India?

A. ₹ 50 crore.

Q. A office colleague happens to receive a pink slip from the company. What does it convey?

A. Job termination letter given to an employee.

Q. A situation develops where wealthy people are in control of running the government. What is the situation described as?

A. Plutocracy.

Q. Bernard Madoff, a US citizen has recently received a jail term of 100 years for indulging in a fraudulent financial scheme. Which is this well known scheme?

A. Ponzi scheme.

Q. Which are those goods which are banned from international trade by countries?

A. Contraband goods.

Q. It is a unique way of defrauding a customer by deducting small amounts from his bank account regularly without being noticed. What is this form of improper practice known as?

A. Salami slicing.

Q. What was the name of the savings bank account which did not prescribe the maintenance of minimum balance?

A. No frills account.

Q. Why were 'no frills accounts' being promoted in India in a big way?

A. For spreading financial inclusion in the country.

Q. The name 'no frills account' has been substituted with a different name. What is the new term?

A. Basic savings bank account.

Q. When joint accountholders of a bank account agree to operate their account on 'E or S' basis what does it suggest?

A. Any one of the joint accountholders can operate their joint account on Either or Survivor basis.

Q. Islamic banking is based on which law?

A. Sharia'h law of Islam.

Q. What does Islamic banking prevent?

A. Earning of interest on money.

Q. Which is the main earning asset of banks?

A. Loans.

Q. Interest on loans from banks in India is linked to a particular benchmark. What is this benchmark?

A. Base rate of lending.

Q. *Dabba* trading is often used in the context of stock markets. What does this term suggest?

A. It basically means trading in a system outside the stock exchange and not routing the deals within the system.

Q. The balance in inoperative accounts of banks is a cause for concern for Reserve Bank of India. Banks have been asked to closely monitor these accounts for reducing the amount and number of inoperative accounts. Which accounts are classified as inoperative accounts?

A. When there is no transaction in a deposit account by the accountholder for a continuous period of more than two years it is classified as an inoperative account.

Q. When a vehicle is financed by a bank what kind of charge does the bank have over the primary security?

A. The charge of hypothecation.

Q. The beginning of the microfinance movement in India could be traced to a pilot project started by NABARD in 1992. Which is this project that is being referred to?

A. Self-help group bank linkage programme.

Q. These are localized associations of members who mobilize funds from among themselves and provide loans from this corpus of funds to their members only. The association is basically for the mutual benefit of the members only. This kind of groups has been in existence since long. What is the name given to such formations?

A. Nidhis.

Q. Another means of informal savings channel comes from a fairly common form of association among different individuals. In this case a particular individual floats a group inviting membership for which a monthly contribution is paid by the person wishing to join. Each month a member can bid for the amount that is collected from the members. The members continue to pay the monthly subscription till each member gets the bid amount once. What is this form which is sufficiently old and is governed by special rules and regulations?

A. Chit funds which are governed by the Chit Fund Act, 1982.

Q. It is considered to be a negotiable instrument by usage and practice only. This instrument has been in use since long for payment of money and comes written in vernacular language. Can you identify the instrument?

A. Hundi.

Q. Reverse mortgage loans are a special lending facility for senior citizens. Which financial institution was the first to launch reverse mortgage loans in India in 2006?

A. Dewan Housing Finance.

Q. Different safeguards are being introduced to protect internet banking in the country. One of them is a virtual keypad. What is this product?

A. It is an online application which substitutes the actual physical keyboard.

Q. When a cheque is issued in electronic form instead of its normal physical form by the use of digital signature it is called an electronic cheque. The electronic cheque is accepted as a negotiable instrument by an appropriate action in 2002. What action was taken?

A. An amendment was made under Section 6 of the Negotiable Instruments Act, 1881.

Q. Which was the first development institution in India which got converted into a bank?

A. ICICI Ltd.

Q. Branches of commercial banks which can undertake foreign exchange business directly as approved by the Reserve Bank of India are known as?

A. Authorized dealers.

Q. Which are the reserves that banks have which act as buffer during the times of crisis?

A. Statutory liquidity ratio.

Q. The Aadhar identification number is issued by the Unique Identification Authority of India. How many digits does the number have?

A. 12.

Q. Which authority in India conducts the economic census for the country?

A. Central Statistical Organization.

Q. As per the extant policy of the Reserve Bank of India, the cash reserve ratio of scheduled banks is fixed at a certain percentage of their NDTL. What is the full form of NDTL?

A. Net Demand and Term Liabilities.

Q. Companies raise money through issue of nonconvertible debentures. How is this mode of mobilizing resources explained?

A. Nonconvertible debentures are medium to long-term debt instruments without the facility of conversion to equity of the company.

Q. By what name is the stock price index of the Tokyo stock market known as?

A. NIKKEI.

Q. When currencies are exchanged at some specific future date but at the prevailing exchange rate as on the date of the deal, what is the practice known as?

A. Forward contract.

Q. Which term is used for money borrowed or lent for a day or overnight?

A. Call money.

Q. Banks offer top up loans to borrowers who maintain a good credit record. What is this top up loan?

A. A part of a retail loan which has been promptly repaid in terms of the loan agreement is again offered as loan to such borrowers.

Q. There is a system in use in certain countries which permits transfer of money from one bank or post office account into another account using a central computer. What is this system known as?

A. Giro transfer.

Q. In Japan over 80,000 biometric ATMs use a less intrusive and rare biometric identification system instead of PIN codes. What is this identification process known as?

A. Finger vein technology.

Q. Name the financial instrument which allows companies to hedge their risks against fluctuations in exchange rates?

A. Currency futures.

Q. Banks often receive orders from the court attaching the balance in the deposit accounts of certain individuals who might be involved in legal disputes. These orders prohibit the bank from allowing the depositor to withdraw the money from the accounts attached. What is this order known as?

A. Garnishee order.

Q. The SARFAESI Act provides for enforcement of security interests for realization of loan dues without the intervention of courts. It also provides for sale of the financial assets by banks/financial institutions. Which agency is permitted to buy these financial assets from banks/FIs?

A. The Act provides for sale of the assets to securitization companies/asset reconstruction companies.

Q. Lok Adalats are an accepted mode for recovery of loan dues from defaulting borrowers by banks as an alternate to law suits. What is the monetary ceiling of cases to be referred to the Lok Adalats organized by civil courts?

A. It has been increased to ₹ 20 lakh from the earlier ceiling of ₹ 5 lakh.

Q. There is generally a stipulation to open escrow accounts by contracting parties till the deal is fully settled. What is the purpose of an escrow account?

A. Escrow account is an account controlled by an intermediary who protects the interests of both buyer and seller in a particular transaction till fulfilment of certain conditions or till the deal is completed.

Q. The system of measurement based on the standard units of ounce, pound and ton is still in use in certain countries. What is this system known as?

A. Avoirdupois.

Q. Islamic finance which prohibits the payment of interest on savings permits the marketing of the financial product 'takaful'. What kind of product/service does this term represent?

A. It is a cooperative or mutual insurance service.

Q. Actuaries prepare these tables according to age, sex and occupation of the individuals. These tables are based on the life expectancy of the population of the country and helps in pricing of life insurance products. What are these tables known as?

A. Mortality tables.

Q. The insurance sector employs agents to market and procure business for the insurance companies. However, agents are prone to quitting their jobs regularly which inconveniences the policyholders as the service gets affected. What are these insurance policies known as?

A. Orphan insurance policies.

Q. At times due to the election process governments at the Centre in India are not able to present the Annual Budget during the scheduled time in February every year. When the regular budget is delayed, an advance grant is made by Parliament. What is this system called?

A. Vote on account.

Q. In case of bouncing of cheques the beneficiary of the cheque has remedy against the drawer of the cheque by filing a criminal case for recovery of the amount of the cheque. What is the solution in case of payments by the electronic mode like electronic clearing service?

A. The beneficiary has similar rights under the Negotiable Instruments Act.

Q. Credit information companies are permitted to collect information about individual/corporate borrowers from banks, financial institutions for sharing the data with their members. Which particular legislation permits this activity in India?

A. Credit Information Companies Act, 2005.

Q. There are at present four well known credit information companies working in India. Which authority is meant to regulate these companies?

A. Reserve Bank of India.

Q. Cheque bouncing is an offence under the Negotiable Instruments Act, 1881. What is the maximum punishment for this offence?

A. Monetary fine of double the cheque amount which has bounced and imprisonment up to two years.

Q. Deposits in banks are insured up to a certain amount. Who pays the premium for this insurance?

A. Individual banks.

Q. What is the source of funds for the International Monetary Fund?

A. Each member nation has to contribute to the IMF.

Q. The word credit is derived from the Latin word which when translated means 'to believe'. Can you mention the Latin word?

A. 'Credere'.

Q. MICR cheques were introduced to expedite the process of clearing of cheques. What does MICR stand for?

A. Magnetic Ink Character Recognition.

Q. The rating of IPOs is mandatory as per the instructions of Securities and Exchange Board of India. How many grades are there in this rating process?

A. Five.

Q. Sweat equity was the reason for an unpleasant controversy in India leading to political resignations. What is the form of this equity?

A. It is a form of equity share given to employees or directors of a company on favourable terms in recognition of their contribution to the company.

Q. Currency of ₹ 1,000 denomination was in circulation earlier also before it was demonetized to fight black money. In which year was this action to demonetize taken?

A. 1978.

Q. The salary and wages an individual receives is for work rendered during a period of time. There is another form of income like dividend payments which are generated without having to directly work for it. What are these forms of income known as?

A. Passive income.

Q. There are two ways in which money can be created or produced. One way is to produce paper currency or mint coins. Which is the other method?

A. By loaning when money gets created.

Q. Divestment as a means to raise resources is often adopted by governments. Which well known economist introduced this concept?

A. Keynes.

Q. In 1993 John Taylor, an economist propounded a rule known as the Taylor's rule which essentially concerns the monetary policy of central banks. What does the rule suggest?

A. It prescribes the degree of change in interest rates made by a central bank in response to the change in inflation and GDP from their expected levels.

Q. The divestment proceeds of minority share holdings of the government in public sector enterprises are deposited in which account?

A. National Investment Fund.

Q. Special Drawings Rights are funding facilities available to members of the International Monetary Fund. These SDRs are allocated to the members in what proportion?

A. It is linked to the country's subscription to the IMF.

Q. The relationship between tax rates and changes in collection of tax revenues is best explained by an economic model. Which is this model?

A. Laffer curve.

Q. The International Accounting Standards Board has developed a set of accounting standards which is steadily becoming the global standard for preparation of financial statements of public companies. What is this accounting standard known as?

A. International Financial Reporting Standards IFRS.

Q. It is known as the core capital of banks and includes equity capital and disclosed reserves. This component of a bank's capital essentially serves the purpose of absorbing losses, if any. What is the technical term for this capital as per Basel regulations?

A. Tier I capital.

Q. It is said that India's wealth around 2020 would be close to US$ 10 trillion. How would you describe 1 trillion as having how many zeroes?

A. 1 trillion has 12 zero.

Q. What is the range band within which the Statutory Liquidity Ratio SLR may be fixed by the Reserve Bank of India?

A. 24 to 40 per cent.

Q. Which is the authority responsible for assessing the risk coverage in life insurance products?

A. Actuary.

Q. What is the book-building mechanism for pricing of public offerings of shares?

A. It offers a price band between which investors can bid for the shares. The issue price is fixed after receiving the responses.

Q. The prime lending rate used by banks for pricing of their loans has been replaced by the Reserve Bank of India. Which was the new rate mechanism introduced?

A. Base rate of lending which will not permit interest rates on loans to be fixed below this rate except a few exempted categories.

Q. In which way can a borrower convert his nonperforming account to a standard loan account?

A. By paying arrears of interest and principal amounts due to the bank.

Q. The Reserve Bank of India mandates that banks must maintain a provision coverage ratio of 70 per cent for its bad loan accounts. What message does it convey?

A. It means that for every ₹ 100 of bad loans ₹ 70 must be set aside as provisions which would take care of loss to the bank in case of write off of the loan.

Q. It is the process of collection of outstation cheques through local clearing. At notified centres this facility is available which expedites the clearing of outstation cheques within two to three days. What is this facility known as?

A. Speed clearing.

Q. A special deposit account with a designated public sector bank can be opened by an individual who wishes to save long-term capital gains tax. The investments have to be routed through such accounts for getting the benefit. Under which scheme can such accounts be opened?

A. Capital gains account scheme.

Q. It is a fixed rate mortgage agreement in which the monthly payments increase over time according to a set schedule. The interest rate on the mortgage does not change during this period. What are such forms of mortgages known as?

A. Fixed rate mortgage.

Q. It is a banking term to denote an account one bank holds with a bank in another country in the currency of that country. It facilitates inter bank payments for the benefit of its customers. What is the name of such accounts?

A. Nostro accounts.

Q. HDFC Bank and ICICI Bank are considered as foreign companies as per the government's regulations though the majority voting rights are with Indians. What is the reason for such classification?

A. ICICI Bank has 77 per cent and HDFC Bank has 64 per cent of their holdings with foreign entities.

Q. Commercial banks are meant to comply with the statutory requirement of 40 per cent priority sector lending annually. What is the penalty for banks not fulfilling this stipulation?

A. Banks not achieving their target of 40 per cent priority sector lending are required to deposit the amount of shortfall in the Rural Infrastructure Development Fund.

Q. A new and novel way of lending has started where lenders can select their particular borrower from a lending platform. The profiles of the prospective borrowers are put up for the choice of the lender. What is this form of lending called?

A. P-to-P or Peer-to-peer lending.

Q. There are credit cards, debit cards and charge cards. What is the special feature of charge cards?

A. It is a card that requires full payment of dues before the end of billing period every month as it does not provide any credit facility beyond the due date of payment.

Q. Aadhar enabled payment system is very much in the news as it is supposed to revolutionize the way India is being governed. What does this system mean?

A. The Aadhar identification number is being used to credit the amount of government subsidies to the account of the eligible beneficiaries.

Q. Certain immovable properties require substantial funds for its maintenance, repairs, payment of property taxes and the total cost exceeds the rental gain from it. Such properties are identified by a special term. What is this word?

A. Alligator property.

Q. It is a secure electronic network used by banks in the US for their financial dealings. It expedites inter bank payments and serves as an alternative to cheque payments. Which is this network?

A. Automated clearing house (ACH).

Q. The MICR code on cheques is a 9-digit figure containing vital information which helps in faster clearance of cheques. Which are the details that it encodes?

A. The 9 digits are further subdivided into the city code (first three numbers) representing the city having the bank account, the bank code (the next three digits) indicating the bank in that city and the branch code (the last three digits) identifying the particular branch of the bank which has the account.

Q. The IFSC number which is an 11-digit alphanumeric code helps identify a bank branch. The first four numbers represent the bank's code. What does the remaining seven digits indicate?

A. A control character (o) and the next six digits for the branch of the bank.

Q. What are the components of Tier II capital also known as secondary capital of a bank?

A. It consists of undisclosed reserves, general loss reserves and subordinated debt.

Q. Capital adequacy ratio to be maintained by banks as part of prudential norms is a percentage of its risk weighted assets. What is risk weighting?

A. Every financial asset carries an element of risk, the extent of which varies. RBI has assigned percentage weights to the degree of risk each category of assets carry.

Q. The major source of income for banks is the interest earnings from their credit portfolio. However, interest charged in certain loan accounts are not to be taken as income by banks. Which are these loan accounts?

A. Accounts which have been classified as nonperforming accounts.

Q. Reserve Bank of India is empowered to regulate the payments systems in India. Which legislation enacted in 2007 gives RBI these powers?

A. Payment and Settlement Systems Act, 2007.

Q. The efficiency of banks is judged on different parameters, one of which is the productivity of employees. How is this element of efficiency calculated?

A. The total business figures of the bank is divided by the total number of employees of the bank which gives the business per employee.

Q. A short-term facility for providing working capital loans is through discounting of bills of the sellers relating to commercial transactions. What is this facility?

A. The bank accepts the bill of exchange as security and advances a percentage of the bill amount to the seller who is the bank's customer.

Q. Virtually every bank Note in the world is printed, at least partially, using this technique because its distinctive appearance and texture make it easier to spot counterfeits. What is this special technique of printing currency notes known as?

A. Intaglio printing.

Q. At times it becomes necessary to attach a sheet of paper to a bill of exchange for the purpose of documenting the endorsements. This attachment is known by a special name. What is it?

A. Allonge.

Q. If a foreign bank was to have an account with an Indian bank in an Indian city, what type of account would it be?

A. Vostro account.

Q. This is a third party service that is actually a system of computer processes that process, verify and accept or decline credit card transactions on behalf of the merchant through secure internet connections. It is the infrastructure that allows a merchant to accept credit card and other electronic payments. Which mechanism are we referring to?

A. Payment gateway.

Q. This mathematical analysis is used to identify the bankruptcy risk of corporations. The result produced is known as Z score. Which analysis is this?

A. Zeta analysis.

Q. Mortgage of immovable property can be done in different ways according to the intention of the parties to contract of borrowing. There is a form of mortgage in which the possession of the mortgaged property is given to the mortgagee, who can retain the said property till his dues are liquidated through the payments accruing to the property by way of rents, etc. Banks do not favour it as the mortgager is not bound in any way regarding his liability to pay the mortgage money. What is this mortgage form?

A. Usufructuary mortgage.

Q. It is a system of banking where banks are permitted to offer a range of services to their customers. Besides the traditional services of deposits and loans, banks also offer investment services. What would you call such banking?

A. Universal banking.

Q. This proposal announced by the US government aims to limit risky behaviour within banks but is narrower than the Glass Steagall Act. Banks taking retail deposits would not be allowed to engage in proprietary trading that is not directly related to the market making and trading they do for customers. This rule was inspired by the former Chairman of Federal Reserve. Can you name this rule?

A. Volcker rule.

Q. High end investment banking institutions that cater to a select clientele have come to be known by this term. It was initially meant for top notch firms like J P Morgan, Goldman Sachs, Mckinsey, etc., but with the fast changes in the economy other big companies are entering this exclusive club. What are we referring to?

A. White shoe investment banks.

Q. Often an exercise of an overall review of a sector or industry is conducted if instances of frauds are noticed in a few companies of that industry. This awareness is due to the need for transparency. What term is used to describe such exercises?

A. Wild catting.

Q. It is a single number which indicates the possibility of bankruptcy of a company within the next two years. A number below 1.8 suggests likely bankruptcy while a score above 3 is considered safe. Which score are we talking about?

A. Z score.

Q. It is a bad debt which is so old that it is probably forgotten by the debtor that it was ever owed. The creditor, of course, has the right to recover the amount provided it is not debarred by the law of limitation. These debts have a special name. What is it?

A. Zombie debt.

Q. RBI is again considering granting of licenses for establishment of private sector banks. When and which bank was the last to get a banking license?

A. YES Bank got the license last in 2002.

Q. It is a special legal provision granted to banks by which they are permitted to produce certified copies of documents in courts instead of the original document. This is an enabling provision to reduce the difficulties/hazards in bringing voluminous banking documents/records to courts. Which is this special privilege for banks?

A. Banker's Book of Evidence.

Q. It relates to the purchase or sale of government securities by the central bank to increase or decrease money supply in the economy. By what name is it known?

A. Is referred to as Open Market Operations (OMO).

Q. 'Hawala' transactions signify illegal transfer of funds and are prohibited under the law. Which law in India prohibits carrying of hawala deals?

A. Foreign Exchange Management Act (FEMA).

Q. They are identified as unscrupulous people who accumulate personal wealth through unfair and unethical means but tend to cover their illegal practices with philanthropic activities. By which term are they identified?

A. Robber Barons.

Q. In modern day living it is the practice of many individuals to provide for living expenses from the income of their fixed investments. Retired persons not having any source of income other than interest income from their investments are a classic example. Such individuals are known by which particular term?

A. Rentiers.

Q. It is a legal entity (trust body) which is established as specified in an individual's will, after his demise. Which is this body?

A. Testamentary trust.

Q. The word was coined after the crises of 2008 in the USA to describe a financial misfortune with undesirable implications. It was the collapse of the investment banking institution Lehman Brothers in the USA which made this term to be coined. What is the term?

A. 'Lehman moment'.

Q. We are referring to the model developed by Arthur Lewis, the Nobel Prize winner in economics who studied the relationship between the farming and manufacturing sector of an emerging economy. It postulates the theory that the agricultural sector provides the labour force to the more dominant manufacturing or industrial sector in an economy at lesser wages till such time the wages rise. The wages rise once the supply of labour declines. This is the turning point when the industrialized sector slows down and growth suffers due to absence of cheap labour. What is the name of this theory?

A. Lewis turning point.

Q. It is an Indian financial messaging standard which is similar to the SWIFT, the international messaging system. This system developed by IDRBT, Hyderabad is to facilitate exchange of secure messages by acting as a platform for intra bank and inter bank applications. What are we talking about?

A. Structured financial messaging system (SFMS).

Q. It includes tangible assets but excludes depreciation, debt and intangible assets. This is what a shareholder would theoretically receive if the company was to be liquidated. What are we referring to?

A. Book value of a company.

Q. USA has held the presidency of the World Bank since its formation while the IMF has similarly been the monopoly of another country/geographical region. Which is that country/region?

A. Europe.

Q. The shadow banking system serves a crucial role in an economy. Which organizations constitute this shadow banking system?

A. Nonbanking financial companies.

Q. Which location in USA is known as the insurance capital of the world?

A. Hartford Connecticut which is the location of some 50 multinational and national insurance companies.

Q. The term demographic dividend is frequently used in the context of economic measures. Which of the following appropriately explains this term?

(*i*) declining crude birth rate

(*ii*) reducing total fertility rate

(*iii*) Increase in life expectancy at birth

(*iv*) Larger percentage of young population and a reducing dependency rate.

A. (*iv*)

Q. Among measures of integration which of the following forms allow free movement of labour and capital among member nations?

(*i*) customs union

(*ii*) economic union

(*iii*) common markets

(*iv*) preferential trade arrangements.

A. (*iii*)

Q. Service tax has become an important source of revenue generation in India. When was this tax first introduced?

(*i*) 1990-91

(*ii*) 1994-95

(*iii*) 1996-97

(*iv*) 1999-2000.

A. (*ii*)

Q. The revenues collected are shared between the Central Government and the State Governments in India on the basis of certain provisions. Which of the following is responsible for formulating these rules?

(*i*) the Central Government

(*ii*) the State Governments

(*iii*) the Planning Commission

(*iv*) the Finance Commission.

A. (*iv*)

Q. 'Supply creates its own demand.' To whom among the following would you attribute this view?

(*i*) Keynes

(*ii*) Adam Smith

(*iii*) J. B. Say

(*iv*) Kenneth Galbraith

A. (*iii*)

Q. In which of the following countries is the Unit Banking system prevalent?

(*i*) India

(*ii*) USA

(*iii*) UK

(*iv*) Canada

A. (*ii*)

Q. With which of the following activities would you associate the term 'plain vanilla currency options'?

(*i*) floating of commercial papers

(*ii*) launch of new mutual fund schemes

(*iii*) dollar rupee exchange rate

(*iv*) fixing the opening price of a share on a particular business day.

A. (*iii*)

Q. In times of economic globalization which is the most advanced type of economic integration?

(*i*) through common markets

(*ii*) free trade area

(*iii*) customs union

(*iv*) economic union.

A. (*iv*)

Q. Money laundering is an issue which engages the mind of most finance professionals. With which of the following statements would you link this issue?

(*i*) hiding of income source mainly to avoid income tax

(*ii*) money acquired through criminal activities

(*iii*) money procured from undisclosed sources and deposited in foreign banks

(*iv*) it is the process to convert money obtained illegally to appear to have originated from legitimate sources.

A. (*iv*)

Q. Financial instruments are transferable through endorsement and delivery. Which of the following cannot be transferred from one person to another by means of endorsement?

(*i*) fixed deposit receipt

(*ii*) cheque

(*iii*) promissory notes

(*iv*) bills of exchange.

A. (*i*)

Q. In case of bank loan accounts against which legal cases have been initiated for recovery of dues, alternate steps are possible to expedite the recovery process. Which of the following action banks may adopt to serve its purpose?

(*i*) Lok adalats

(*ii*) one time settlements

(*iii*) action under the SARFAESI Act

(*iv*) all of the above.

A. (*iv*)

Q. Banks are meant to adhere to approved standards and codes in discharge of their lending responsibilities. The lending process is meant to be transparent and the borrower is supposed to be aware of his rights and duties. In this regard which is the code that banks are required to follow?

(*i*) Banking Ombudsman code

(*ii*) Consumer Protection code

(*iii*) Fair Practices code for lenders

(*iv*) None of the above.

A. (*iii*)

Q. The global economy is witness to countries engaging in currency wars. What is the reason behind countries adopting this posture?

(*i*) countries manoeuvre exchange rates to improve their trade

(*ii*) balance of payments are disturbed by countries with strong currencies

(*iii*) counterfeit currency is floated by countries to weaken the other country

(*iv*) inferior goods are exported by countries with strong currency to kill the domestic markets of the weaker countries.

A. (*i*)

Q. The success of their maiden public issues make the companies go for FPOs. What purpose does an FPO serve?

(*i*) these are follow on public offers for further issue of shares

(*ii*) follow on offers dilute the holding of the subscribers to IPOs

(*iii*) FPO gives additional shares to those successful in the maiden issue

(*iv*) An FPO is issued when additional funds are required.

A. (*i*)

Q. SFIO or Serious Fraud Investigation Office is an important wing of the government which is investigating certain companies accused of financial irregularities. Which of the following explain their area of investigation?

(*i*) company law violations having multidisciplinary issues

(*ii*) financial irregularities in the banking sector

(*iii*) frauds of more than ₹ 10 crore in the financial sector

(*iv*) corporate frauds in collusion with banks.

A. (*i*)

Q. Hedging and speculation are common activities in the foreign exchange market. Which of the following options would you equate with these two activities?

(*i*) these are parallel activities

(*ii*) these are opposite activities

(*iii*) these are similar actions

(*iv*) all of the above.

A. (*ii*)

Q. Which of the following would best explain a currency swap?

(*i*) a forward sale of currency together with a forward repurchase of the same currency through two different transactions

(*ii*) a forward sale of currency along with a forward repurchase of the same currency as part of a single deal

(*iii*) a spot sale of currency with a forward repurchase of the same currency as part of a single transaction

(*iv*) none of the above.

A. (*iii*)

Q. Which of the following legal regulations has defined the word 'banking'?

(*i*) Negotiable Instruments Act, 1881

(*ii*) Reserve Bank of India Act, 1934

(*iii*) Banking Regulation Act, 1949

(*iv*) Banking Companies (Acquisition and Transfers of Undertakings) Act, 1970.

A. (*iii*)

Q. 'Crossing' is an important aspect to safeguard payments of instruments. Crossing is applicable to which of the following instruments?

(*i*) promissory notes

(*ii*) cheques

(*iii*) fixed deposit receipts

(*iv*) bills of exchange.

A. (*ii*)

Q. Which of the following funding mechanisms would not qualify as a long-term source of finance?

(*i*) equity shares

(*ii*) preference shares

(*iii*) debebture and bonds

(*iv*) fixed deposits.

A. (*iv*)

Q. What is the current method that banks use for calculating and paying interest in savings bank accounts?

(*i*) on monthly products based on minimum balance between the 10th and the last working day

(*ii*) product of daily balance is calculated and interest paid accordingly

(*iii*) on average quarterly balance

(*iv*) interest not paid where the daily balance falls below the minimum required balance.

A. (*ii*)

Q. While calculating income earned from loan accounts which of the following accounts are excluded by banks for this purpose?

(*i*) substandard accounts

(*ii*) doubtful accounts

(*iii*) standard accounts

(*iv*) only (*i*) and (*ii*).

A. (*iv*)

Q. With which of the following statements would you link a revocable letter of credit?

(*i*) can be cancelled by the issuing bank without the consent of the beneficiary

(*ii*) can be cancelled by the issuing bank with the consent of the beneficiary only

(*iii*) can be cancelled by permission of RBI

(*iv*) can be cancelled only if the buyer's bank agrees.

A. (*i*)

Q. An international organization publishes regularly an annual report known as the 'Doing Business Report'. Which is this organization?

(*i*) World Trade Organization

(*ii*) World Bank

(*iii*) International Monetary Fund

(*iv*) Organization for Economic Cooperation and Development.

A. (*ii*)

Q. The financial sector laws in India are being revised in view of rapid changes that have taken place in this sector over the years. Which of the following authorities has been given the task of rewriting these very old laws?

(*i*) Financial Stability Development Council

(*ii*) Reserve Bank of India

(*iii*) Financial Sector Legislative Reforms Commission

(*iv*) The Finance Ministry.

A. (*iii*)

Q. Banks allow borrowing against pledge of goods. Which statement would you say best explains an agreement of pledge of goods?

(*i*) the ownership of the goods remain with the borrowers but the possession is passed on to the bank

(*ii*) the ownership of the goods is passed on to the bank but the possession remains with the borrower (*iii*) both the ownership of the goods and possession remain with the borrower

(*iv*) the bank is in possession of the goods and ownership.

A. (*i*)

Q. If the exchange rate quotations are based on foreign currency as the fixed unit and the exchange rate varies in terms of home currency, such quotations are known as?

(*i*) direct quotations

(*ii*) indirect quotations

(*iii*) foreign currency quotations

(*iv*) none of the above.

A. (*i*)

Q. When equitable mortgage of an immovable property is executed what process is followed?

(*i*) the mortgage deed is registered with the Registrar's office

(*ii*) the mortgage deed is registered under the Transfer of Property Act

(*iii*) the mortgage deed is executed by the borrower with two witnesses and the deed is deposited with the bank

(*iv*) the borrower delivers to the bank the title deeds of his immovable property with an intention to create an equitable mortgage as security.

A. (*iv*)

Q. Banks exercise their right of lien in cases where the customer has a loan outstanding and deposits in his name with the bank. What would be a case of negative lien?

(*i*) a declaration of the borrower to the effect that his assets are free from encumbrances and that he shall not use them as security or dispose them without the bank's permission

(*ii*) a special type of lien on the shares of public limited companies

(*iii*) a right of the bank to take possession of all assets hypothecated to the bank in case of default by the borrower

(*iv*) none of the above.

A. (*i*)

Q. The term 'multicurrency basket' is often used in financial transactions. What does it mean?

(*i*) a number of international currencies to which the value of Special Drawing Rights is linked

(*ii*) selected international currencies to which the value of the Asian monetary unit is linked

(*iii*) number of major international currencies to which the external value of the Indian rupee is linked

(*iv*) the name given to a select group of European currencies.

A. (*iii*)

Q. A transaction which leads to an outflow of foreign currency would qualify as?

(*i*) selling transaction

(*ii*) buying transaction

(*iii*) forward transaction

(*iv*) futures transaction.

A. (*i*)

Q. Which one of the following would *not* be considered as a salient feature of debit cards?

(*i*) works like a normal withdrawal slip

(*ii*) no interest earning for banks

(*iii*) 30 days credit facility available to the cardholder

(*iv*) No bad debt for banks.

A. (*iii*)

Q. An existing bank account of a resident in India who goes overseas for gainful employment and for an uncertain period will be termed as?

(*i*) non-resident account

(*ii*) blocked account

(*iii*) non-resident foreign currency account

(*iv*) inoperative account.

A. (*i*)

Q. In case of lending, borrowers permit *pari passu* charge of their assets. What does it mean?

(*i*) a charge which would have priority to any other charge, existing or future

(*ii*) equally and without any partiality between two lenders

(*iii*) a charge which would have the last priority to any other charge, existing or future

(*iv*) a charge which does not require any registration.

A. (*ii*)

Q. Among different forms of mortgage there is scope for creating mortgage through the process of an English mortgage. What is this form of mortgage?

(*i*) registration of charge with the Registrar

(*ii*) transfer of title to the creditor with condition that on payment of the loan the title will be transferred back to the owner or mortgagor

(*iii*) deposit of title deeds with the creditor with the intention of creating a mortgage

(*iv*) handing over possession of the property to the creditor.

A. (*ii*)

Q. A revolving letter of credit would be best explained by which of the following statements?

(*i*) utilized value automatically gets reinstated after payment of bills already drawn

(*ii*) the credit facility can be transferred from one seller to another seller

(*iii*) once a bill is paid, reinstatement to the extent of 50 per cent takes place

(*iv*) merchandise quality goes on changing freely.

A. (*i*)

Q. Uniform Customs and Practice for Documentary Credits UCPDC is an international code regulating the operations of bankers' documentary letters of credit. Which authority has issued it?

(*i*) International Monetary Fund

(*ii*) International Chamber of Commerce

(*iii*) US Federal Reserve

(*iv*) The UN.

A. (*ii*)

Q. Underwriting a public issue of shares implies that the bank would straightaway:

(*i*) apply for shares

(*ii*) apply only when the issue is not subscribed to fully

(*iii*) not apply at all

(*iv*) ask the staff to buy up shares.

A. (*ii*)

Q. Which of the following institutions mobilize the savings of the general public to invest in the industrial and manufacturing sector?

(*i*) Unit Trust of India

(*ii*) General Insurance Corporation

(*iii*) Life Insurance Corporation

(*iv*) All of the above.

A. (*iv*)

Q. Which of the following would not be regarded as a source of funds of a commercial bank?

(*i*) capital

(*ii*) deposits

(*iii*) cash reserves with RBI

(*iv*) call money borrowings.

A. (*iii*)

Q. A savings bank accountholder has made a nomination in his account. In a situation where the accountholder is unwell, the nominee wants to operate the account. What is the bank required to do?

(*i*) bank will permit the nominee to operate the account

(*ii*) as the nominee is a close relative, the bank will permit him to operate the account

(*iii*) because of very cordial relations with the accountholder, the bank will allow the nominee

(*iv*) as nomination is effective only in the event of death of the accountholder, the bank will not allow.

A. (*iv*)

Q. A jointly owned property is to be equitably mortgaged to the bank. The mortgage can be executed:

(*i*) only by all the jointholders

(*ii*) any of the jointholders

(*iii*) any of the jointholders authorized by all

(*iv*) jointly owned properties cannot be equitably mortgaged.

A. (*i*)

Q. After much thought RBI has agreed to the introduction of White Label ATMs in the country. With which statement would you associate these White Label ATMs?

(*i*) they are so named because they are white in colour

(*ii*) these ATMs are managed by nonbanking finance companies

(*iii*) these are jointly owned by two or more banks

(*iv*) these ATMs are imported from the European coun ies.

A. (*ii*)

Q. Which branches of commercial banks in India are competent to handle foreign exchange business?

(*i*) only metro branches

(*ii*) branches in state capitals

(*iii*) branches designated as authorized dealers

(*iv*) all branches are permitted.

A. (*iii*)

Q. FCNR(B) accounts of non-resident Indians can be opened in which of the following currencies?

(*i*) pound sterling

(*ii*) US dollars

(*iii*) Euro, yen, Swiss francs

(*iv*) All of the above.

A. (*iv*)

Q. Special Drawing Rights or SDRs which is the currency of the International Monetary Fund is in which of the following forms?

(*i*) paper currency

(*ii*) gold

(*iii*) silver coins, bars

(*iv*) bookkeeping entry only.

A. (*iv*)

Q. Which of the following can be an underlying asset for a derivative?

(*i*) equity

(*ii*) interest rate

(*iii*) commodities

(*iv*) all of the above.

A. (*iv*)

Q. Derivatives as a financial instrument was first used as a tool for which of the following activities?

(*i*) speculation

(*ii*) hedging

(*iii*) volatility

(*iv*) arbitraging.

A. (*ii*)

Q. Whenever RBI engages in transactions known as the Open Market Operations, which of the following activities is it attempting to influence?

(*i*) liquidity in the economy

(*ii*) inflation

(*iii*) borrowing powers of banks

(*iv*) flow of foreign investments.

A. (*i*)

Q. The actual return of an investor is reduced when the prices of the commodities show an upward trend suddenly. What is this type of effect known as?

(*i*) probability risk

(*ii*) market risk

(*iii*) inflation risk

(*iv*) credit risk.

A. (*iii*)

Q. How would you interpret the logo of State Bank of India?

(*i*) a key hole

(*ii*) a circle with the common man in the centre

(*iii*) key to the bank

(*iv*) none of the above.

A. (*ii*)

Q. Name the country which has decided to stop issue and payment of cheques from October 2018 and that all payments should be made and accepted in electronic form only?

(*i*) USA

(*ii*) Russia

(*iii*) France

(*iv*) UK.

A. (*iv*)

Q. Banks in India do not entertain request for loans against the security of the bank's own shares. Why is it so?

(*i*) it is prohibited by RBI

(*ii*) it is not permitted by the Banking Regulation Act

(*iii*) it is against the provisions of the Companies Act

(*iv*) it is considered risky.

A. (*ii*)

Q. Which of the following is not a document of title to goods as per law and practice?

(*i*) bill of lading

(*ii*) airway bill

(*iii*) Warehouse receipt

(*iv*) Bill of exchange.

A. (*iv*)

Q. The Lead Bank scheme for public sector banks does not cover:

(*i*) metropolitan cities

(*ii*) all states and union territories

(*iii*) backward districts

(*iv*) rural areas only.

A. (*i*)

Q. A bank assumes different roles of creditor, debtor, agent while dealing with customers. When does the bank perform the role of lessor?

(*i*) in cash dealings

(*ii*) when accepting articles for safe custody

(*iii*) when renting out locker

(*iv*) when executing a mortgage deed.

A. (*iii*)

Q. When there is transfer of immovable property there is often reference to mutation. What does mutation mean?

(*i*) deposit of title deeds with the bank

(*ii*) cancellation of any mortgage facility previously availed

(*iii*) recording of transfer of property from one person to another in the revenue records

(*iv*) payment of registration charges for the property.

A. (*iii*)

■■■

QUIZ FOUR

MONEY, FINANCE AND BANKING-II

Q. What do you understand from the word BIFR?

A. Board for Industrial and Financial Reconstruction.

Q. With which types of industries would BIFR be linked?

A. Sick industrial units.

Q. IRDA is meant to regulate which sector of the Indian economy?

A. Insurance.

Q. What is the financial year for Reserve Bank of India?

A. July to June.

Q. Finance Commissions in India are constituted after how many years?

A. After every 5 years.

Q. What is the scope of Finance Commissions?

A. The distribution of financial resources between the Centre and States in India

Q. With which financial sector in India would you associate RuPay with?

A. The payments and settlement system.

Q. National Small Savings Fund manages which types of investments?

A. Small savings schemes.

Q. RTGS is a mechanism to achieve what?

A. Fund transfers between bank accounts on real time basis.

Q. NEFT is a parallel facility to which well known alternative?

A. Telegraphic transfer of funds.

Q. How would you classify ECS?

A. Electronic Clearing Service.

Q. Which institution qualifies as the bankers' bank in India?

A. Reserve Bank of India.

Q. With which type of banking products is a DSA employed?

A. Retail loan and deposit products.

Q. What is the feature of misselling?

A. The practice of financial institutions, banks to sell a product without describing its features truly and appropriately.

Q. Bank rate in India is decided by which institution?

A. Reserve Bank of India.

Q. Fiscal policy of an economy relates to which economic activity?

A. The declaration of the financial policy and management of finances of a country by its government.

Q. Foreign exchange reserves of India are in which form?

A. Gold and foreign currency.

Q. India's money market deals in which instruments?

A. In instruments for overnight investment and up to one year.

Q. FDI in the Indian economy refers to which type of money flow?

A. Long-term capital investment.

Q. Scheduled banks in India are those banks:

(*a*) which are nationalized by the Central Government

(*b*) which are selected by the Reserve Bank of India

(*c*) which are included in the Second schedule to the RBI Act, 1934

(*d*) which participate in the payments and settlements system

A. (*c*)

Q. Who pays the insurance premium for deposit insurance in banks?

(*a*) the customer

(*b*) the respective banks

(*c*) the Central Government

(*d*) RBI

A. (*b*)

Q. The term banking has been defined in which Act?

(*a*) Banking Regulation Act, 1949

(*b*) Negotiable Instruments Act, 1881

(*c*) RBI Act, 1934

(*d*) Banking Companies (Acquisition and Transfer of Undertakings) Act, 1970

A. (*a*)

Q. Currently public sector banks in India are required to lend .....% of their total advances to the priority sector?

(*a*) 32

(*b*) 36

(*c*) 40

(*d*) 42

A. (*c*)

Q. The Government of India contributes ....% of the share capital of regional rural banks?

(*a*) 15

(*b*) 35

(*c*) 40

(*d*) 50

A. (*d*)

Q. The amount of deposit in a customer's account in banks in India insured by DICGC is?

(*a*) ₹ 50,000/-

(*b*) ₹ 1,00,000/-

(*c*) ₹ 2,00,000/-

(*d*) No limit

A. (*b*)

Q. Which of the following is not a long-term source of finance?

(*a*) preference shares

(*b*) debentures

(*c*) fixed deposits

(*d*) equity

A. (*c*)

Q. The authority of Exchange Control in India rests with?

(*a*) Foreign Exchange Dealers Association of India

(*b*) Finance Ministry

(*c*) RBI

(*d*) Indian Banks Association

A. (*c*)

Q. Which is the international code for regulating documentary letters of credit in cross-country trade?

(*a*) General Agreement on Trade and Tariffs

(*b*) Uniform Customs and Practices for Documentary Credits

(*c*) UN charter on trade

(*d*) IMF protocol

A. (*b*)

Q. What method does RBI follow while issuing currency notes?

(*a*) fixed fiduciary system

(*b*) proportionate reserve system

(*c*) maximum reserve system

(*d*) minimum reserve system

A. (*d*)

Q. The basic difference between visible exports and visible imports is known as?

(*a*) terms of trade

(*b*) revenue deficit

(*c*) balance of trade

(*d*) balance of payments

A. (*c*)

Q. Regional rural banks area of operation in India is?

(*a*) entire state

(*b*) district where it is located

(*c*) a few blocks in the district

(*d*) the entire state

A. (*b*)

Q. The National Bank for Agriculture and Rural Development is?

(*a*) an independent bank

(*b*) a sectoral bank of RBI

(*c*) a department of the Finance Ministry

(*d*) under the Agriculture Ministry

A. (*a*)

Q. Which of the following is not the responsibility of the central bank of a country?

(*a*) framing monetary policy

(*b*) acting as banker to banks

(*c*) dealing with foreign exchange

(*d*) controlling government spending

A. (*d*)

Q. The National Financial Switch is the key element in electronic payments. What type of payments does it facilitate?

(*a*) internet banking
(*b*) ATM payments
(*c*) Mobile banking
(*d*) Electronic clearing services

A. (*b*)

Q. Which of the following is the main purpose of having the 'Know Your Customer' guidelines for financial institutions?

(*a*) to keep a check on money laundering
(*b*) to have better customer service
(*c*) to bring more people under the tax net
(*d*) to expedite high value transactions

A. (*a*)

Q. Finances are distributed between States and the Centre in India on the recommendations of which of the following?

(*a*) National Development Council
(*b*) Planning Commission
(*c*) Finance Commission
(*d*) Public Accounts Committee

A. (*c*)

Q. The term IRR used in banking and financial sectors in the context of credit refers to which of the following?

(*a*) internal revaluation reserve
(*b*) internal rate of return
(*c*) investment reserve ratio
(*d*) internal risk return

A. (*b*)

Q. What is cross-border exchange?

(*a*) hawala trading of Indian rupee
(*b*) illegal transfer of Indian rupee
(*c*) foreign exchange trade in India
(*d*) dealing in counterfeit currency

A. (*a*)

Q. Regarding the International Monetary Fund which of the following is correct?

(*a*) it can grant loans to any country
(*b*) it can grant loans to only developed countries

(*c*) it can give loans to only member countries

(*d*) it provides loans to the central bank of a country.

A. (*c*)

Q. All revenues received by the Union Government by way of taxes and other receipts for the conduct of government business are credited to which account?

(*a*) Contingency Fund of India

(*b*) Consolidated Fund of India

(*c*) Deposit and Advances Fund

(*d*) Public Account.

A. (*b*)

Q. The lowering of Bank Rate by the Reserve Bank of India leads to which situation?

(*a*) more liquidity in the market

(*b*) less liquidity in the market

(*c*) no change in the liquidity position in the market

(*d*) mobilization of more deposits by commercial banks.

A. (*a*)

Q. Both Foreign Direct Investment FDI and Foreign Institutional Investor FII are related to investment in a country. Which one of the following statements best represents an important difference between the two?

(*a*) FII helps bring better management skills and technology while FDI only brings in capital

(*b*) FII helps in increasing capital availability in general while FDI only targets specific sectors

(*c*) FDI flows only into the secondary market while FII targets the primary market

(*d*) FII is considered to be more stable than FDI.

A. (*b*)

Q. Financial sector reforms in India consist of which of the following?

(*a*) lowering of CRR and SLR

(*b*) entry of private firms in the insurance sector

(*c*) deregulation of rate of interest

(*d*) all of the above.

A. (*d*)

Q. Which one of the following is not an instrument of fiscal policy?

(*a*) public revenue

(*b*) public expenditure

(*c*) public borrowing

(*d*) cash reserve ratio.

A. (*d*)

Q. Consider the following statements:

(*a*) credit creation varies inversely with cash reserve ratio

(*b*) credit creation varies positively with cash reserve ratio

(*c*) bond price and interest rate are inversely related

(*d*) bond price and interest rate are directly related

which of the above statements are true?

(A) a and c (B) a and d (C) b and c (D) b and d.

A. (A)

Q. Which of the following is not considered as a money market instrument?

(*a*) treasury bills

(*b*) commercial papers

(*c*) repurchase agreements

(*d*) certificates of deposit.

A. (*c*)

Q. When the rate of inflation increases

(*a*) purchasing power increases

(*b*) purchasing power decreases

(*c*) value of money increases

(*d*) purchasing power remains unaffected.

A. (*b*)

Q. In terms of its definition Special Drawing Rights (SDRs) are a monetary unit of the reserve assets of which of the following organizations?

(*a*) International Monetary Fund

(*b*) World Bank

(*c*) Reserve Bank of India

(*d*) Federal Reserve.

A. (*a*)

Q. The most popular measure of inflation in India is

(*a*) wholesale price index

(*b*) consumer price index

(*c*) general price rise

(*d*) dearness allowance rates.

A. (*a*)

Q. Which of the following is the most important component of the liabilities of commercial banks in India?

(*a*) demand deposits

(*b*) time deposits

(*c*) inter bank liabilities

(*d*) other borrowings.

A. (*b*)

Q. Land development banks in India form part of:

(*a*) commercial banks

(*b*) IDBI

(*c*) FCI

(*d*) Cooperative credit structure.

A. (*d*)

Q. Consider the following statements with regard to Statutory Liquidity Ratio (SLR):

(*a*) to meet SLR commercial banks can use cash only

(*b*) SLR is maintained by the banks with themselves

(*c*) SLR restricts the banks' leverage in pumping more money into the economy.

Which of the statement(s) given above is/are correct?

(A) a, b and c

(B) a and b

(C) b only

(D) b and c.

A. (D)

Q. Which of the following terms is e-commerce?

(*a*) B2B

(*b*) B2C

(*c*) C2C

(*d*) All of the above.

A. (*d*)

Q. On stock exchanges which of the following are transacted:

(*a*) only securities

(*b*) only commodities

(*c*) listed securities only

(*d*) commercial papers.

A. (*c*)

Q. Shares can be issued:

(*a*) at par

(*b*) at discount

(*c*) at premium

(*d*) all of the above.

A. (*d*)

Q. The debentureholders of a company are company's:

(*a*) owners

(*b*) creditors

(*c*) customers

(*d*) all of the above.

A. (*b*)

Q. The functions of SEBI includes:

(*a*) registration of market players

(*b*) regulation of primary and secondary markets

(*c*) protection of investors

(*d*) all of the above.

A. (*d*)

Q. The important credit rating agencies working in India are:

(*a*) CRISIL

(*b*) CARE

(*c*) ICRA

(*d*) All of the above.

A. (*d*)

Q. A nonbanking financial company owes its existence to which of the following:

(*a*) Banking Regulation Act, 1949

(*b*) Negotiable Instruments Act,1881

(*c*) Companies Act,1956

(*d*) Reserve Bank Act.

A. (*c*)

Q. Deposit Insurance Credit Guarantee Corporation reports to which of the following authorities:

(*a*) Finance Ministry

(*b*) IRDA

(*c*) RBI

(*d*) Is independent.

A. (*c*)

Q. A country's current account is not likely to have which of the following components?

(*a*) remittances

(*b*) dividend returns

(*c*) foreign investments

(*d*) trade figures

A. (*c*)

Q. When there is net withdrawal of currency from currency chest by banks what is the impact on the money circulation in the economy?

A. There would be expansion in the supply of currency.

Q. It is a small device that goes over the card reading slot in an ATM machine and reads the card's magnetic stripe. In this way the scammers are able to commit frauds in the credit card accounts. What is this device commonly known as?

A. ATM skimmers.

Q. Currency notes in India are exchanged in terms of the RBI (Note Refund) Rules. There are a particular set of currency notes which cease to be a legal tender if it carries some message and thus claims on them are rejected. What is the definition of such messages?

A. Any note with slogans and messages of a political nature written across it ceases to be a legal tender.

Q. There might be a supplement to a will, containing an addition, explanation, and modification, etc., of something in the will. What is the name given to such supplement?

A. Codicil.

Q. All investments in markets rise and fall over time and is referred to as volatility. To overcome this obvious feature, investors keep investing on a regular basis to absorb both the rise and fall in the markets. This method of investing which neutralizes the volatility is known by a special term. What is it?

A. Rupee cost averaging.

Q. The demand for rating of small and medium enterprises is on the rise as it helps in getting bank funding. There is an agency which exclusively rates units from the SME sector. Which is this agency?

A. SME Rating Agency of India Ltd., SMERA

Q. These products from mutual funds were part of tax savings schemes. They had a lock-in period of three years and invested in stocks. Which schemes are we talking about?

A. Equity linked savings schemes

Q. It is an agreement between two parties to exchange interest payments and principal on loan denominated in two different currencies. The loans would have to be of equal value.

What is this agreement called?

A. Cross-currency swap.

Q. The term is used to denote the number of times an unit of money in an economy changes hand during a particular period of time. It is calculated by dividing the value of gross domestic product with the value of money in circulation. What is it that we are looking at?

A. Velocity of money.

Q. This mechanism handles ATM transactions. It is a router that reads a debit/credit card and routes the request to the respective bank's servers. What is the name of this router?

A. National Financial Switch.

Q. It is possible that an ATM may read the credit/debit card and process the transaction correctly, yet it may not disburse the cash. Why?

A. There may not be cash available in the ATM bins.

Q. It is regarded as the eighth largest corporate bankruptcy in US history and the biggest securities firm to go bust since Lehman Brothers in 2008. The company had placed bets on bonds floated by Italy, Spain, Belgium, Portugal and Ireland but the move back fired. It also had a subsidiary in India. Which is this failed company?

A. MF Global Holdings Ltd.

Q. As part of financial regulators its mandate is to promote the growth of warehousing business in India. How is this regulator known as?

A. Warehousing Development and Regulatory Authority WDRA.

Q. Private banks were allowed in India as a result of the liberalization process set in by the Narasimham Committee report in the 1990s. Number of banks was established but soon thereafter mergers and acquisitions started taking place. HDFC Bank kicked off by acquiring in 1999 one of the new entrants in the banking sector. Which was the bank that was acquired?

A. Times Bank.

Q. It is a form of electronic money denominated in gold weight. The typical unit of account for such currency is the gold gram or the troy ounce, although other units such as gold dinar are sometimes used. What is this type of currency known as?

A. Digital gold currency.

Q. It is an economic system where powerful business groups use their access to the political class to dominate the economy. It is denoted by a special term. Can you name the term?

A. Crony capitalism.

Q. It is a bond which has had its coupons removed. The holder of this bond is entitled to its par value on maturity but not to the annual interest payments. What is this type of bond called?

A. Strip bond.

Q. It is probably the oldest form of rehabilitation which consists of an agreement between an insolvent debtor and his creditors under which the creditors agree to accept an amount less than the total of their claims. This amount is supposed to be distributed *pro rata* to all the creditors in discharge of the entire debt. What is this form of settlement called?

A. Composition settlement.

Q. Investments by means of participatory notes are not favourably accepted as it is felt that these notes are being misused to rig the stock market with unaccounted funds from overseas. How is investment through participatory notes pushed into the country?

A. These are derivative instruments that allow foreigners to invest in Indian stocks through brokers without registering with the Indian authorities.

Q. In a stock buyback or 'stock repurchase' a company buys back its shares from its share holders. What happens to the repurchased shares?

A. The repurchased shares are cancelled thereby bringing down the number of existing shares.

Q. Predicate offence refers to any offence as a result of which proceeds generated from transactions may become the subject matter of an illegal act. Under which law such predicate offences are covered?

A. Prevention of Money Laundering Act.

Q. Tare weight is a term used in documents linked to shipping. What does it signify?

A. It is the weight of a shipment excluding the goods being shipped, *i.e.,* the weight of the shipping container.

Q. A holder of a watered stock is in an unenviable position. He does not know what to do with the stock. Why?

A. It is the ownership of a company whose total worth is less than its capital investment.

Q. Sukuk bonds are fairly popular in Malaysia, Dubai and Bahrain. What is the special feature of these bonds?

A. These are Islamic bonds structured to comply with principles of Shariah law which prohibits the charging or paying of interest.

Q. The microfinance institutions have formed a self-regulatory body for development of the industry on professional lines. The members cover most of the big and prominent micro finance companies which are keen to regulate their working. What is this organization called?

A. Micro Finance Institutions Network (MFIN).

Q. DICGC established in 1962 is the second oldest deposit insurance agency in the world. What is the main source of income for DICGC?

A. The premium paid by the banks on their deposits.

Q. Arbitrage is known as stock trading on two different exchanges at different prices. What then is statistical arbitrage?

A. It is a strategy used by traders to benefit from differences in prices of two or more financial instruments that are related or similar in nature.

Q. It is a method of investing used by wealthy investors and companies who want exposure to a variety of products such as equities, fixed income, gold and structured products. Such facility is not available to a mutual fund. What is this form of investing known as?

A. Portfolio management services.

Q. Where is the National Financial Switch located in India and which organization has developed it?

A. NFS is based in Hyderabad and it has been developed by the Institute for Development and Research in Banking Technology.

Q. There is an investment strategy which involves creating an income ladder, by creating one step at a time. An amount of ₹ 5 lakh can be split into ₹ 1 lakh and invested yearly in one, two years blocks and so on. In what way is this strategy known?

A. Laddering strategy.

Q. It refers to the sale of receivables to a financial company for liquidity needs. The company gets a percentage of the total receivables from the institution which buys the receivables. What is this mechanism called?

A. Factoring.

Q. Inventory management and its efficiency is reflected by this ratio. It is an indicator of the rate at which the inventory is turned into accounts receivable. A lower ratio implies an efficiently managed inventory. Which financial ratio is being discussed?

A. Inventory turnover ratio.

Q. There is a life insurance plan in which the insurance amount becomes payable to the beneficiary when the insured dies within a specified period. There is no payment if the insured is alive at the end of the policy period. What is the name given to these insurance plans?

A. Term life insurance.

Q. There are instances when the subject matter of insurance is insured with two or more insurers and the total sum exceeds the actual value of the subject matter. What would you call such insurance?

A. Double insurance.

Q. There is a specific term used to describe the amount that is given off by way of reinsurance. It is the amount accepted by the reinsurer. Which is this term?

A. Cession.

Q. In case payment of premiums on an insurance policy is discontinued after premium is paid for the first three years the amount payable by the insurer is reduced. What is this amount known as?

A. Paid-up value.

Q. If the policyholder surrenders his right under a policy before its maturity and terminates the contract, what is the amount that is paid?

A. Surrender value.

Q. It is a comprehensive Act designed to protect the interests of consumers by providing redressal mechanisms for settlement of grievances. Banking and other financial services are covered under this Act of 1986. Which is this Act?

A. Consumer Protection Act, 1986.

Q. This Act is the first legislation governing all forms of insurance which gives the state strict control over insurance business. Name the legislation?

A. Insurance Act, 1938.

Q. Government promoted funds of foreign countries is exploring business opportunities in India. They have substantial resources for investment. What are these funds known as?

A. Sovereign wealth funds.

Q. Most commercial banks in India have voluntarily signed the code prepared by the Banking Codes and Standards Board of India. The code spells out the standards that banks are required to establish and follow while discharging their services to customers. By what name is the code known?

A. Code of Commitment by Banks to Customers.

Q. Four multinational banks in the UK agreed to pay a total of 9 billion pounds sterling to their customers who were probably missold an insurance product. Which was this insurance product?

A. Payment protection insurance (PPI).

Q. There is a rule of thumb which says that about 20 per cent of consumers in a product category accounts for about 80 per cent of sales. It is referred to as the 80/20 principle. What is the name of this theory?

A. Pareto principle.

Q. Name the security printing press which prepared the seal of the Reserve Bank of India?

A. Security printing press at Nasik.

Q. It is a free trade agreement signed between the countries of US, Canada and Mexico. Name this agreement?

A. NAFTA North American Free Trade Agreement.

Q. ATMs handle innumerable transactions daily of a diverse number of customers. In what way does an ATM identify the customer?

A. The customer identity is verified from the magnetic code on the card and the password in the form of PIN which is keyed in by the customer.

Q. Banks are permitted by RBI to issue these instruments as smart cards, magnetic strip cards, internet accounts, mobile wallets which facilitate purchase of goods and services against value stored on such instruments. The value represents the value paid for by the holders either by cash or transfer from accounts. What are these instruments called?

A. Pre-paid instruments.

Q. The Central Government is regularly recapitalizing the public sector banks with huge funds. Why is this necessary?

A. To enable the banks to meet their capital adequacy ratios and for growth of business.

Q. The process of recapitalization of public sector banks started in the mid-1990s. Why was this not required earlier?

A. In the mid-1990s prudential norms were adopted by RBI for compliance by banks which meant fulfilling the capital adequacy ratio and provisioning for stressed assets.

Q. Net interest margin (NIM) and spread are two key parameters that indicate a bank's operational efficiency. How is NIM determined?

A. Net interest margin is arrived at by dividing a bank's net interest income by its average interest earning assets.

Q. The small savings schemes of the government offered through the post offices have undergone a revision with regard to the interest rates applicable on them. They remained fixed for considerable length of time without any revision. What changes have been made in this regard?

A. Government now notifies interest rates on these schemes at the beginning of every financial year based on the average yields on government securities of similar maturity with a positive spread of 25 basis points.

Q. The Fiscal Responsibility and Budget Management Act (FRBM) enacted in 2003 had proposed changes in the management of fiscal policy. What were the proposals?

A. The proposals were to eliminate revenue deficit by 2008-09 and to have a 3% limit on fiscal deficit after 2008-09.

Q. Service tax was launched in 1994 when only 3 services were identified for taxation. As of financial year 2011-12, 119 services were in the tax net and as of Budget 2012-13, 150 services are targeted. What is the criterion for choosing the services to be taxed?

A. All services will be taxed unless covered in negative list or otherwise exempted.

Q. What is the share of service tax in the total revenue collection from taxes of the government as per estimates of 2011-12?

A. 11.50% is the share of service tax in the total tax collection.

Q. According to asset classification norms in force in banks what is a standard asset?

A. Standard assets are those where borrowers pay their interests on the loans as per the loan repayment schedule.

Q. How would you classify those loan accounts which have remained nonperforming for a period less than or equal to 12 months?

A. Substandard assets.

Q. What is the criteria for terming a loan account as nonperforming?

(*a*) An account where a borrower fails to pay the interest on the loan for three consecutive months

(*b*) Where the borrower does not get his account inspected after every three months

(*c*) An account where the interest is not paid for two consecutive quarters

(*d*) Only (*a*) and (*c*)

A. (*a*)

Q. If an account has remained as a substandard asset for 12 months how is it classified?

A. As doubtful asset.

Q. Banks and auditors treat such accounts as loss for the bank where chances of recovery of the loan amount is remote. What kind of nonperforming accounts is it known as?

A. Loss assets.

Q. In case of foreign banks which do not meet the target of 32% lending to the priority sector what is the penalty imposed by Reserve Bank of India?

A. The shortfall has to be deposited with SIDBI.

Q. Credit Default Swap (CDS) is a derivative instrument that is becoming increasingly popular in the financial market. What is/are its special features?

(*a*) Transfers the risk element from investors to risk absorbers for a fee

(*b*) It improves investment and borrowing opportunities by redistributing risk

(*c*) In a way it promotes credit flow and thereby liquidity

(*d*) All of the above.

A. (*d*)

Q. For housing loans up to ₹ 15 lakh interest subvention of 1% is offered by the government to promote housing for the lower and middle sections of the society. What is this interest subvention?

A. Interest subvention is a financial incentive as it enables a borrower to source a loan at lower interest rates.

Q. Advocates generally prepare these reports after visiting the registrar's office and inspecting the property documents. The title certificate issued thereafter indicates whether the property is free from encumbrances. The report acts as a security for the purchase of a property. What report are we referring to?

A. Search report traces the history of a property like who was the original owner and who have been the subsequent buyers till the time of search.

Q. Kisan credit card is like an overdraft facility to be operated by the farmer. The kisan credit card scheme was introduced in 1998. Which authority administers this scheme?

A. NABARD.

Q. SEBI was not in existence then when RBI granted the merchant banking license to this bank sometime in late 1960s. Which bank was this?

A. Grindlays Bank.

Q. It is an institution that is engaged in the business of issuing management either by making arrangements regarding selling, buying or subscribing to securities as manager, consultant, advisor or rendering corporate advisory services in relation to such issue management. What is the name given to such institutions?

A. Merchant Bank.

Q. This is a social security scheme of the government which was started in 1952 for the working class and meant to provide tax-free retirement savings. Employees and employers contribute regularly to the fund every month and on retirement the employee gets a lump sum amount and monthly pension thereafter. What is this scheme known as?

A. Employees' Provident Fund.

Q. It is a contract between the bank or financier and the customer for financing of capital equipments. The customer has possession of the asset and makes payment of specified rentals and other charges to the bank/lender who remains the owner of the asset. This arrangement provides for 100% finance without margin requirements which is different from term loans. What type of financial transaction is it known as?

A. Financial lease.

Q. The assets created by the finance are taken as security and the cash flow generated from the project is the source of funds for repaying the project loan. It is meant for financing large capital intensive programmes with long gestation periods. What are we referring to?

A. Project financing.

Q. This is an arrangement whereby banks can borrow funds from RBI at 1% above the liquidity adjustment facility – repo rate against pledge of government securities. This facility for banks is in cases of substantial shortfall of liquidity and to check short-term asset liability mismatches. What is the name of this facility?

A. Marginal standing facility MSF.

Q. A customer has multiple fixed deposits with a bank but the total interest earned by him on these deposits is not paid by the bank. Why is it so?

A. Interest earned on bank fixed deposits is subject to tax deducted at source.

Q. These are additional life covers apart from the basic cover for a comprehensive protection. It essentially means covering other risks which are not part of the main life policy. There is an extra cost for the additional protection provided through this facility. What are these additional risk covers known as?

A. Riders to an insurance policy.

Q. Third party administrators assist in settling insurance claims of the insured and also provide services to get the best treatment at the right price. Who are the third party administrators?

A. They are entities who work as intermediaries between insurance companies and health care providers.

Q. A period of fifteen days is allowed by insurance companies to the policy buyer to confirm acceptance or rejection of his decision to buy an insurance policy. If the customer decides to change his decision to buy, the insurance policy can be returned. This is a customer-friendly initiative introduced by the insurance regulator. What is the special name for this time given to the customer to make a decision?

A. Free look period.

Q. Why do public sector banks regularly present dividend cheques to the Central Government?

A. The majority shareholders of public sector banks is the government and hence when profits are declared the government as the biggest beneficiary is paid the dividend.

Q. This institution was set-up in 1987 as a wholly-owned subsidiary of the Reserve Bank of India. The function of this institution is to operate as the principal agency to promote housing finance institutions at the local and regional levels. It is also responsible for ensuring stability in the housing finance market. It also introduced the concept of reverse mortgage scheme meant for senior citizens. Identify the institution?

A. National Housing Bank.

Q. This body coordinates the various important activities of the banking industry in the country. It was set-up in 1946 with 22 members to meet the diverse needs of the member banks. A change in its rules in 1990 enabled the financial services industry and other related units to join as associate members. It also participates in the wage settlements for employees of the public sector banks. Can you identify this organization?

A. Indian Banks' Association.

Q. The clearing house operations have got further boost with CTS or Cheque Truncation Services which has expedited the clearing process and is more secure. What is the main feature of this service?

A. It sends electronic image of the cheques for clearing instead of the physical cheque.

Q. The depositor may nominate a person to whom the bank may make the payment of the balance in the deposit account in the event of his death. This benefit of nomination is not available in which of the following accounts?

(*a*) partnership accounts

(*b*) joint accounts

(*c*) senior citizens accounts

(*d*) minor accounts.

A. (*a*)

Q. The IFO Business Climate is a widely observed early indicator for economic development. It is based on approximately 7,000 monthly survey responses of firms in manufacturing, construction, wholesaling and retailing business. In which country is this indicator in use?

A. Germany.

Q. This organization is known for fighting corruption. 'Corruption Perception Index' is published by them which rates countries according to the degree of corruption that is prevalent in them. Which is this organization?

A. Transparency International.

Q. It is considered as a slang term for describing women who run their own business while also acting as a full-time parent. Can you name the term?

A. Mompreneur.

Q. It is a word coined by management consultant Gifford Pinchot for an employee who displays entrepreneurial skills in a large firm without incurring the risks associated with those activities. What is that word?

A. Intrapreneur.

Q. Thomas Carlyle referred to the subject of economics as 'Dismal Science' in relation to the hypothesis that starvation would result as projected population growth exceeded the rate of increase in food supply. Which particular model did he have in mind in this regard?

A. The Malthusian model.

Q. In the book 'Boomerang' Michael Lewis mentions that this country was shown as No. 1 in the UN's 2008 Human Development Index but ironically in October 2008 it was effectively a bankrupt nation. Which country is he referring to?

A. Iceland.

Q. Which commodity is considered to be the most traded commodity in the world?

A. Crude oil.

Q. The 'Dependency Ratio' is an age to population ratio of those not usually forming the labour force. Which is the age band that it excludes from the dependency factor?

A. The age band of 15 to 64 years.

Q. One can know the approximate time it would take to triple one's money if that particular figure is divided by the estimated interest rate. What is that figure?

A. 114 divided by the interest rate indicates the time required to triple one's money.

Q. If the quotation for a bond's price is inclusive of interest, what term is usually used to denote this fact?

A. Dirty price.

Q. Historically planned economy as used in World Bank terminology is meant to describe which type of countries?

A. Refers to the second world countries attempting to turn into market economies.

Q. General Anti Avoidance Rules (GAAR) relate to legal provisions which serve as a deterrent against tax avoidance transactions. The GAAR provisions which suitably empower the tax authorities created much controversy in India lately. What do these rules relate to?

A. To declare any arrangement as impermissible if the same is intended to result in certain tax benefits to the parties involved in a transaction.

Q. Hundis were accepted as a financial instrument through practice and usage but is not a negotiable instrument. What do you call a hundi which is payable to the name mentioned or to his order and is considered similar to an order cheque?

A. 'Firman jog hundi'.

Q. The term indicates a fixed amount which is charged as fees or commission for rendering particular type of services. This method is preferred to charge of variable fees which are mentioned on percentage basis. The method of charging of the fees is generally incorporated in the contract for the services. What is this term?

A. Flat dollar.

Q. It refers to the sale of export receivables, where an enabling company discounts the receivables of an exporter against fees for the service. It means converting the sale of goods by an exporter for which funds are awaited, into cash. Usually the enabling company bears the risk in case of default of payment by the importer. The word is derived from the French language meaning 'give up our right'. What is this service or facility known as?

A. Forfaiting.

Q. The Reserve Bank of India has issued instructions which stipulate that banks should have a dedicated back up manager for each wealth management customer in addition to the one who is officially assigned. If interpreted figuratively the rule implies that four eyes would be watching the transactions. What is the name given to this rule?

A. Four eyes principle.

Q. It concerns the principle of holding a reserve by the bank which is a small fraction or percentage of the total deposits held by the bank. This model is the basis of banking in India. What is this principle known as?

A. Fractional reserve banking.

Q. It represents the online facility of contributing/donating money to temples and charitable organizations. Well known temple authorities in India have provided the facility for making these payments. What is the facility called?

A. Known as e hundi.

Q. Those regularly in need of borrowing prefer this short-term loan which instead of being adjusted is periodically renewed. What type of loan is it?

A. Evergreen loan.

Q. This is a hundi payable at sight and could be considered as similar to a demand bill. The hundi must be presented for payment within a reasonable time after its receipt by the holder. By what name is it known?

A. Darshani hundi.

Q. Debtor velocity is an important ratio for the banks in deciding the quantum of loan to be given to the company. What information do the banks derive from this ratio?

A. Indicates the average collection period or the period of credit given by a company.

Q. Dhannijog hundi is a demand bill of exchange payable only to the dhanni. This instrument was treated as not negotiable. Who is the 'dhanni'?

A. The payee.

Q. For foreign banks in India the rating model used by Reserve Bank of India is a modified version of the model used for Indian banks. The rating is an annual exercise to assess the strengths in the identified areas. What is the model known as?

A. Known as CACLS, it is – C for capital adequacy, A for asset quality, C for compliance, L for liquidity and S for systems and controls.

Q. A practice has evolved whereby commercial banks engage in unduly speculative or risky financial activities to record high profits. It has the tendency to indulge in excessive financing of activities in the real economy. This high risk business has attracted a particular name. What is this form of banking called?

A. Casino banking.

Q. Chapter 7 is the chapter of the US Bankruptcy Reform Act, 1978 which prescribes the guidelines to be followed in case a company in the US is facing financial crisis and seeks to redress the situation. Which eventuality does it cover?

A. It applies to cases for voluntary liquidation.

Q. These provisions of the US Bankruptcy Reform Act, 1978 seeks to protect a company in financial distress from its creditors, who demand its liquidation. The provisions in the particular chapter enable the stressed company to open negotiations with its creditors for a viable reorganization of its business for improving its financial position. Can you identify the provisions which are frequently mentioned in the context of financially weak companies?

A. Chapter 11 provisions.

Q. We are referring to the practice adopted by individuals who own properties in more than one country. They are required to execute separate wills for these properties as a matter of convenience and for simplifying matters. What term denotes this practice?

A. Concurrent will.

Q. This banking word is understood to be derived from the Latin word *'credere'* meaning 'to believe'. Can you name it?

A. Credit.

Q. Investors transacting in shares and other listed securities on a recognized stock exchange require this important document. It is basically a legal record of transactions carried on a stock exchange. Which is this important document?

A. Contract note.

Q. Banks are permitted to invest in various capital instruments like stocks and bonds issued by public and private sector companies and commercial papers. However, these investments are not considered by Reserve Bank of India for computation of an important ratio. Which is this ratio?

A. Statutory liquidity ratio.

Q. IFRS is a set of accounting standards developed by the body known as IASB to make it globally acceptable for preparation of financial statements of public companies. What is this IASB agency?

A. International Accounting Standards Board which is an independent group of 15 experts.

Q. The forced exit of GMR Infrastructure from Maldives recently caused a huge loss to the Indian company. It is felt that GMR could have easily cut its losses if it had taken an insurance policy to cover losses arising out of adverse political developments in foreign countries where they have projects for execution. What is this insurance cover called?

A. Political risk cover.

Q. The abolition of monetization has led to significant increases in market borrowings of the governments. What is the system that has been put in place?

A. Government bond auctions.

Q. Developed countries used quantitative easing to push growth following the 2008 financial crisis. What constitutes quantitative easing?

A. Central banks push money directly into the economy by buying government securities or other securities from the market.

Q. The Unit Trust of India was the first mutual fund set-up in India. Which institution was responsible for its establishment?

A. Reserve Bank of India.

Q. ARDC is credited with the first major venture capital success story when its investment in Digital Equipment Corporation in 1957 yielded great returns after a few years. What was the full form of ARDC?

A. American Research and Development Corporation.

Q. This model of management practices places excessive reliance on positive thinking. What is the term used for this particular type of leadership?

A. Prozac leadership.

Q. RBI has permitted the setting up of white label ATMs in India. There is yet another class of ATMs in which the hardware as well as the lease of the machine is under ownership of the service provider. The connectivity, cash handling and management is the responsibility of the bank. What are these ATMs called?

A. Brown label ATMs.

■■■

QUIZ FIVE

Capital Markets

Q. Financial markets need regulation for effective functioning. Who is the regulator for stock markets in India?

A. Securities and Exchange Board of India – SEBI.

Q. Which authority is the stock market regulator in UK?

A. Financial Services Authority FSA.

Q. Which is the oldest stock exchange in India?

A. Bombay Stock Exchange – BSE.

Q. What does the acronym DJIA in the context of stock trading mean to you?

A. Dow Jones Industrial Average which is quoted on the New York Stock Exchange.

Q. Which is the first public sector share to be quoted on the Bombay Stock Exchange?

A. Hindustan Petroleum Corporation.

Q. Which famous doyen of the capital markets is the founder of the National Stock Exchange?

A. R. H. Patil.

Q. If someone were to mention the term 'Chalu Upla' while discussing stock trading what would it mean?

A. It is an unofficial deal, one which is not made on the floor of the stock exchange.

Q. In stock exchange trading what is indicated by ALGO?

A. Algorithm trading.

Q. Bulls and bears is common terminology in the stock markets. How did it originate?

A. When the markets move up it resembles bulls who attack in an upward motion and bears attack with their paws down indicating a downward movement.

Q. Which is India's first exchange to go for an IPO and get listed on the stock exchanges?

A. Multi Commodity Exchange MCX.

Q. Which is the oldest stock exchange in the Asian continent?

A. The Bombay Stock Exchange (BSE) which was started in 1875.

Q. London Stock Exchange was one of the earliest to adopt electronic trading. In which year was it started?

A. In 1986.

Q. There could be a phase in the stock market when it is neither bullish nor bearish. What is this trend known as?

A. Chicken market.

Q. What are illiquid stocks which do not observe the stock market guidelines in India called?

A. Z stocks.

Q. When was the stock market index 'sensex' constituted?

A. In 1979.

Q. Which financial event of serious concern made the Government of India to set-up SEBI?

A. The stock market scam of 1992 initiated by the stock broker Harshad Mehta.

Q. 'Outcry' is a word used to mean a mode of communication in the stock markets. What is this method?

A. It is a method of communicating between professionals on a stock exchange which involves shouting and the use of hand signals to transfer information about buy and sell orders.

Q. Which is the first stock exchange in the world?

A. Amsterdam Stock Exchange.

Q. This first stock exchange traded in the stocks of which well known company?

A. Dutch East India Company.

Q. What is the full form of NSE?

A. National Stock Exchange.

Q. When was NSE established in India?

A. 1994.

Q. Every stock exchange has an index. What is the index of NSE known as?

A. Nifty.

Q. What is the KOSPI index about?

A. It is the Korean Composite Stock Price Index.

Q. When companies approach the stock markets for the first time with their shares what is it called?

A. Initial Public Offering (IPO).

Q. How does an IPO help a company?

A. It helps raises funds for the company by issuing shares to the public.

Q. Which was the first IPO to be issued in India?

A. The Dutch East India Company which was formed in 1602 is considered to have been the first modern company to issue an IPO in early 17th century.

Q. Wall Street is commonly referred to in financial markets. What is it famous for?

A. The financial district in New York, USA where the New York Stock Exchange is also located.

Q. What is NYSE?

A. New York Stock Exchange.

Q. What is the informal name for NYSE?

A. Big Board.

Q. In the context of the London stock exchange what does 'Big Bang' mean?

A. It refers to the change in practices on the London Stock Exchange with the introduction of electronic trading.

Q. How did Wall Street get its name?

A. It was due to a wall ordered to be built there for protection against attacks from the English.

Q. How would you describe an investor who takes interest in new companies?

A. Venture capitalist.

Q. The business world is witness to mergers, takeovers, amalgamations, etc. What would a 'black knight' mean to you?

A. A company which makes a hostile takeover bid for a company which does not want to be bought.

Q. With which individual or an entity would you associate the word 'carey street'?

A. To be heavily in debt or bankrupt.

Q. What does a bear hug in stock market parlance mean?

A. The stock market is seeing a downward trend in stock prices.

Q. In a bull run in the market what happens to the shares?

A. The stock prices are regularly rising.

Q. How would you describe NASDAQ?

A. National Association of Securities Dealers Association.

Q. Hang Seng index is well known. Which market does it represent?

A. The Hongkong Stock Exchange.

Q. What is the full form of ASBA?

A. Application Supported by Blocked Account.

Q. How does ASBA help an investor?

A. The account of the investor is debited only when allotment of shares takes place.

Q. The word 'circular file' is often heard in modern day offices. What does this word indicate?

A. The wastepaper bin.

Q. The NAV of a mutual fund can be associated with which of the following?

(*a*) Increases at a gradual rate

(*b*) Fluctuates with stock market price movements

(*c*) Tends to fall during the bull phase of a stock market

(*d*) Remains constant in value over time.

A. (*b*)

Q. What does the acronym ULIP stand for?

A. Unit Linked Insurance Plan.

Q. e-series is an unique investment product strategy launched by National Spot Exchange Limited in India. Which are the investment products that are being offered through this mechanism?

A. e-gold and e-silver.

Q. Among prominent price indices in the world is the Brent index. To which sector does it relate?

A. Crude oil prices.

Q. Name the sporting personality who rang the closing bell at NASDAQ to commemorate India's 66th independence day?

A. Anil Kumble.

Q. Every financial services segment in India has an independent regulator. Forward Markets Commission is the regulator for which segment?

A. Commodities Futures Market.

Q. When Indian companies raise funds from overseas markets what is the process known as?

A. Foreign currency convertible bonds.

Q. Why does the balance sheet 'balance'?

A. It is because of the concept of double entry bookkeeping, whereby every financial transaction results in an equal change in assets or liabilities.

Q. He was an Italian monk who was associated with debits, credits and double entry accounting approximately 500 years ago. Who was this personality?

A. Pacioli.

Q. Which stock exchange was selected by Facebook for its maiden listing of shares?

A. NASDAQ in the US.

Q. Certain fund schemes invest primarily in government securities. How are these mutual funds known as?

A. Gilt edged funds.

Q. If an investor is to buy zero coupon bonds what would be its price at the time of purchase?

A. The zero coupon bond is bought at a price lower than its face value which is paid on maturity.

Q. Inexperienced first time investors in the stock markets are known by a slightly derogatory term. What is this special term?

A. Aunt Millie.

Q. There are instances when new products of a company overwhelm the existing older products in terms of their production and sales. What is this phenomenon known as?

A. Cannibalization.

Q. An effective way of raising funds for charitable causes has been discovered recently whereby supporters of the cause come together to raise resources. The social media is an important tool in this raising of donations. How is this process defined?

A. Crowd funding.

Q. There are instances when an entity borrows money to lend it further at a profit by taking advantage of a short-term rise in interest rates. What term is used to describe this practice?

A. Round tripping.

Q. Which term is used to define the exchange rate of one currency for another currency over a fixed period of time?

A. Currency swap.

Q. It denotes the acquisition of a company by another by directly approaching the company's shareholders without reaching an agreement with the management of the target company. In such kind of deals the target company does not want the deal to materialize. What term would you use to describe this deal?

A. Hostile takeover.

Q. Mutual funds are set up in the form of trusts which have trustees, asset management companies and custodian. What is the role of the asset management company among these players?

A. The asset management company manages the funds by making investments in different types of securities.

Q. When an issue of securities is made to a select group of persons not exceeding 49 in number by the company and the issue is neither a rights nor a public issue, what is it called?

A. Private placements.

Q. The first ever bell ringing ceremony was performed in the Bombay Stock Exchange in 2002. For which company was this done?

A. Bharti Airtel.

Q. Which was the first Indian company to list its Global Depository Receipts in the Singapore Stock Exchange?

A. Uttam Galva Steels.

Q. American Depository Receipt is an instrument to raise resources. Who can issue an ADR?

A. An Indian company wanting to raise funds in the American market.

Q. Fixed maturity plans are suggested as a good investment option while comparing with fixed deposit schemes. What are fixed maturity plans?

A. These are schemes floated by mutual funds and come in short-term maturities. They invest in investments of matching maturities but do not offer assured returns.

Q. A way of comparing the performance of stocks is to check the amount of dividend yield being paid by the companies. How is dividend yield of stocks understood?

A. The dividend per share divided by the current market price of the share gives the dividend yield of the stock.

Q. It is a ratio that calculates the number of times the actual dividend could be paid out of current year profits. How is this ratio known?

A. Dividend cover.

Q. We often hear of market capitalization of companies on the stock exchange. It is reported to fluctuate according to the sentiments of the market. What do we understand from this term?

A. It means the market value of the outstanding stocks of the company.

Q. SEBI is considering allowing listed companies greater flexibility in structuring deals through the use of options. What is the meaning of options in the financial context?

A. It is a contract that gives the buyer the right, but not the obligation, to buy or sell an asset at or before some particular date at an agreed price.

Q. Pass through certificates (PTC) are issued by banks or finance companies through the process of securitization as it generates additional resources for them. What do you understand about pass through certificates?

A. These certificates are created on conversion of a loan to an investible debt instrument such as bonds and debentures.

Q. At times there are instances in the stock market when a individual investor or company purchases large number of shares of other companies against the wishes of that company. It is generally for gaining a controlling interest in the targeted company or to resell the shares for a higher profit. What name is assigned to these entities?

A. Corporate raider.

Q. The government manages to raise capital from the markets through an autonomous body which acts like an investment banker. Which important organization discharges this responsibility?

A. Public debt office.

Q. It is known as a coefficient to measure equality. The figure of zero signifies absolute equality, whereas figure one denotes gross inequality. Which is this coefficient?

A. Gini coefficient.

Q. Which is the index used to detect the bullish or bearish trend in the stock market?

A. Advance decline index.

Q. If a company in the US is filing Chapter 11 what does it indicate?

A. Filing for bankruptcy.

Q. SEBI in India is the regulator for capital markets in India. Which is the government agency which performs the same task in USA?

A. Securities and Exchange Commission SEC.

Q. Which was the world's first mutual fund on offer?

A. Massachusetts Investors Fund in the USA.

Q. Manhattan is considered as the financial nerve centre of New York. Of which city would you consider Pudong to be a similar equivalent?

A. Shanghai where Pudong is the location for Shanghai stock exchange and important finance and trade centres.

Q. The Hoover index in economics represents the share of the total community income that would have to be redistributed to have perfect equality in the society. It is also known by another name which is a character from popular folklore. What is this term?

A. The Robin Hood index which is conceptually one of the simplest inequality index used in econometrics.

Q. Sensex is the stock index for BSE in India, which market does DAX index represent?

A. It is the index for Frankfurt stock exchange.

Q. Initial Public Offerings offer opportunities for investors to multiply their wealth. Some IPOs are issued with great hype to arouse investor interest and to get the issue over-subscribed. Which particular IPO in India entered the market with the media describing it as 'Black Gold'?

A. The IPO of Coal India.

Q. The price to earnings or P:E ratio is an important indicator in stock market analysis. What does it convey?

A. It is arrived at by dividing the current market price of a share by the earnings per share. It helps investors to decide whether to invest in a stock or not.

Q. Securities and Exchange Board of India (SEBI) was established after the stock market scandal of 1992. Which government agency was performing the task of SEBI earlier?

A. Controller of Capital Issues.

Q. The Native Stock and Share Brokers' Association was formed in 1887. It has come a long way since then and is still surviving to be an active player in the financial markets. How do we know this association today?

A. Bombay Stock Exchange.

Q. How is the New York commodities market that deals in futures of crude and heating oil, leaded petrol, platinum and palladium commonly known as?

A. NYMEX New York Mercantile Exchange.

Q. International rating agencies announce their ratings of different countries based on multiple criteria. The signals sent to the international community differ according to the ratings. What do these sovereign ratings indicate?

A. The creditworthiness of national governments are assessed by taking into account their ability to payback debt after considering economic, market and political risks.

Q. Since these sovereign ratings convey a definite message, what are the types of ratings issued?

A. The ratings generally are under three categories of negative, stable and positive outlook.

Q. Which apex Indian body was set-up in 1927 as an industry representative on the recommendations of Mahatma Gandhi?

A. Federation of Indian Chambers of Commerce and Industry (FICCI).

Q. The Strait Times Index is the stock market index of which country?

A. Singapore.

Q. The names of private limited and public limited companies usually end with the word 'limited'. A company name with 'Berhad' at the end meaning 'limited' would belong to which country?

A. Malaysia.

Q. Which company/institution is known to have made the world's largest public offer worth around US dollar 20 billion in 2006?

A. Industrial and Commercial Bank of China Ltd.

Q. An innovative rural marketing model 'e-Choupal' was introduced by a well known company in India. Which company are we talking about?

A. ITC.

Q. The Government of India has recently introduced a new index called CRIS. It is based on Moody's ratings and data on the GDPs of different nations as given by the IMF. What is the full form of CRIS?

A. Comparative Index for Sovereigns.

Q. NASDAQ is well known as the electronic trading exchange in the USA. Which is the only Indian company to be a part of the NASDAQ 100 index?

A. Infosys.

Q. As part of market liberalization when did the exchange rates become market determined in India?

A. 1993.

Q. Black Monday is often cited as an instance of an extremely adverse market event. This day is regarded as the 19th October, 1987. What really happened on this day?

A. The Dow Jones Industrial Average plunged 23 per cent on a single day.

Q. A Greek business man known as the 'Don' on the international poker circuit was recently sentenced to 7 years in jail by UK courts for defrauding banks to borrow US $1.2 billion. The bank in question was the Allied Irish Bank. Who is this infamous personality?

A. Achilleas Kallakis.

Q. These convertible bonds are different to regular convertible bonds as the likelihood of these bonds converting to equity is contingent on a specified event. For example, the contingent event could be linked to the stock price of the company exceeding a particular level for a certain period of time. What are these convertible bonds known as?

A. Coco bonds.

Q. This term is derived from Latin words 'com' meaning together and 'merx' meaning goods. Which is this word?

A. Commerce.

Q. What would you call a buyout where an investor, typically a financial sponsor, acquires a controlling interest in a company's equity and where a significant percentage of the purchase price is financed through borrowings?

A. Leveraged buyout.

Q. What do you understand from the use of 'greenshoe option' in a share issue?

A. It is a price stabilizing mechanism in which shares are issued in excess of the issue size by a maximum of 15 per cent.

Q. If it is told that Tadawul is the stock exchange of a country, which country would it be?

A. Saudi Arabia.

Q. Islamic finance prohibits the payment of interest on financial instruments. What is the term used for this concept?

A. Riba.

Q. In ancient times Christians denounced the practice of usury as it was considered a sin. What does usury mean?

A. The payment of interest on financial instruments.

Q. Which one of the following financial instruments would qualify as a capital market instrument?

(*a*) Government securities

(*b*) Shares of listed companies

(*c*) Loans and advances

(*d*) Treasury bills.

A. (*b*)

Q. Sensex the stock index of the Bombay Stock Exchange is calculated using which of the following methods?

(*a*) Market turnover

(*b*) Market capitalization

(*c*) SEBI guidelines

(*d*) IFRS mandated rules.

A. (*b*)

Q. Which of the following entities cannot act as a trader in the call money market?

(*a*) State Bank of India

(*b*) SBIMF

(*c*) STC

(*d*) MMTC

A. (*b*)

Q. In the context of various financial systems which of the following is not related to India?

(*a*) RTGS

(*b*) CTS-10

(*c*) NEFT

(*d*) CHAPS.

A. (*d*)

Q. Which of the following defines the amount on shares actually demanded by the company?

(*a*) Subscribed capita

(*b*) Called up capital

(*c*) Authorized capital

(*d*) Issued capital.

A. (*b*)

Q. What name is given to the prospectus issued by the company while approaching the markets with its initial public offering?

(*a*) Blue sky

(*b*) Green shore

(*c*) Red herring

(*d*) Golden parachute.

A. (*c*)

Q. Capital markets regulators are responsible for protecting the interests of investors. Which of the following activities is completely prohibited by the regulators?

(*a*) Margin trading

(*b*) Short sell

(*c*) Insider trading

(*d*) Delisting.

A. (*c*)

Q. Participatory notes as a means to an investment are associated with which of the following?

(*a*) Qualified institutional buyers

(*b*) Foreign institutional investors

(*c*) Peer-to-peer lending

(*d*) Crowd funding.

A. (*b*)

Q. Which of the following types of issues would not be considered as a private placement?

(*a*) Preferential allotment

(*b*) Preference shares

(*c*) Qualified institutional placement

(*d*) Both (*a*) and (*c*).

A. (*b*)

Q. Which of the following appropriately defines the role of registrars to an initial public offering?

(*a*) They carry-out the due diligence to prepare the offer document

(*b*) They are involved in finalizing the basis of allotment

(*c*) They undertake to cover the anticipated subscription to the issue

(*d*) All of the above.

A. (*b*)

Q. Which is the largest stock exchange in the world in terms of dollar value of its listed companies?

(*a*) Chicago stock exchange

(*b*) Stockholm stock exchange

(*c*) New York Stock Exchange

(*d*) FTSE.

A. (*c*)

Q. Which of the following cities is generally considered to be the first to have a stock exchange?

(*a*) Egypt

(*b*) New York

(*c*) Amsterdam

(*d*) Copenhagen.

A. (*c*)

Q. The total number of shares that a company can sell under the provisions of the company's Article of Incorporation is defined by a specific term. Which of the following satisfies this explanation?

(*a*) issued shares

(*b*) outstanding shares

(*c*) preference shares

(*d*) authorized shares.

A. (*d*)

Q. TRIPS is an agreement linked to which of the following issues?

(*a*) Free market economy

(*b*) Human rights

(*c*) Intellectual property rights

(*d*) Political asylum.

A. (*a*)

Q. With which of the following statements would you link the term 'capital structure'?

(*a*) The choice between equity and debt

(*b*) The time needed to repay the debt

(*c*) The kind of assets the firm should invest in

(*d*) Whether the firm invests in capital budgeting projects.

A. (*a*)

Q. There is a means of extending an unsecured loan by one company to another. Which of the following best explains this practice?

(*a*) Commercial paper

(*b*) Intercorporate deposits

(*c*) Treasury bills

(*d*) Certificate of deposits.

A. (*b*)

Q. MCX is the index of which of the following stock exchanges of India?

(*a*) National Stock Exchange

(*b*) Multi Commodity Exchange

(*c*) Bombay Stock Exchange

(*d*) Delhi Stock Exchange.

A. (*b*)

Q. Where and when was the first stock ticker machine used?

(*a*) New York in 1867

(*b*) Frankfurt in 1862

(c) London in 1862

(d) Paris in 1855.

A. (a)

Q. The board of directors of a company is meant to represent which of the following groups?

(a) The top management

(b) The stakeholders

(c) The shareholders

(d) The customers.

A. (c)

Q. What practice did the New York Stock Exchange request listed companies to adopt in 1895?

(a) Registering securities with federal regulators

(b) Issuing an annual report to shareholders

(c) Disclosing executive pay

(d) Reporting stock trades by company executives.

A. (b)

Q. Which of the following is not a service provided by financial markets to corporations?

(a) payment services

(b) managing risk through contracts

(c) liquidity

(d) real investments.

A. (d)

Q. What is the change in status of an investor when he buys stocks of a company?

(a) He becomes a part of the company

(b) Liable for the company's debt

(c) He is likely to be paid the original investment amount with interest by the company

(d) He has advanced money to the company.

A. (a)

Q. Commercial paper is regarded as a short-term security to raise funds. Which of the following institutions issue this particular security?

(a) Reserve Bank of India

(b) State Governments

(c) National Stock Exchange

(d) Large Companies.

A. (d)

Q. If an investor prefers to buy bonds of a company rather than invest in stocks which of the following would describe the situation?

(*a*) He becomes a part of the company

(*b*) He gets to vote on shareholders' resolutions

(*c*) He is liable for the company's debt

(*d*) He has given money to the company as debt.

A. (*d*)

Q. Which of the following authorities has been given the powers to regulate the micro-finance industry in India?

(*a*) SIDBI

(*b*) NABARD

(*c*) RBI

(*d*) SEBI.

A. (*c*)

Q. According to IRDA's extant rules, insurance companies can approach the markets with their IPOs after being in operations for a specified length of time. What is this time stipulation?

(*a*) 10 years

(*b*) 15 years

(*c*) 5 years

(*d*) 25 years.

A. (*a*)

Q. The FTSE 100 index is used to measure the performance of stocks. In which country does it operate?

(*a*) France

(*b*) UK

(*c*) Germany

(*d*) Canada.

A. (*b*)

Q. With which of the following would you identify a Gold Panda in China, Maple leaf in Canada, Philharmonics in Austria and George the Victorious in Russia?

(*a*) Bank account names

(*b*) Gold bullion coins

(*c*) Images on local currency

(*d*) Nick names for banks.

A. (*b*)

Q. Who do you think gets the interest amount in a joint account?

(*a*) Both

(*b*) The first named

(*c*) The applicant

(*d*) The owner of the funds.

A. (*a*)

Q. In 1981, a strike by this labour union placed a severe strain on national infrastructure in the US. The then President Ronald Reagan broke this strike and this action was considered a touch stone in 20th century labour relations. The strike of which labour union was broken?

(*a*) United Auto Workers

(*b*) National Postal Mail Handlers Union

(*c*) The United Transportation Union

(*d*) The Professional Air Traffic Controllers Organization.

A. (*d*)

Q. What would you call a financial intermediary which is in the principal business of buying and selling of securities?

(*a*) Equipment leasing company

(*b*) Hire purchase company

(*c*) Loan company

(*d*) Investment company.

A. (*d*)

Q. There is a need to raise capital for the company whose stocks are already listed on the stock exchange. The company does not intend to increase the number of shares in circulation. Which of the following should the company adopt to achieve its objective?

(*a*) Rights issue

(*b*) Stock split

(*c*) Bond issue

(*d*) Open offer.

A. (*c*)

Q. Apart from common stock being listed on the stock exchanges it may be traded in which of the following ways?

(*a*) Over the counter

(*b*) Between directors of the company

(*c*) Between officials of the company

(*d*) By brokers who own an inventory of shares from which they buy/sell.

A. (*a*)

Q. In which of the ways can an investor buy bonds?

(*a*) On the stock markets

(*b*) Through an investment fund

(*c*) On the money markets

(*d*) Directly from shops.

A. (*b*)

Q. In which of the following assets would the nomination of the owner make the nominee the actual beneficiary in the event of his death and not remain merely as the custodian?

(*a*) bank deposits

(*b*) equity shares

(*c*) mutual funds

(*d*) life insurance policy.

A. (*b*)

Q. Gold exchange traded funds are alternative investments options for the public. Which of the following statements may be identified as features of gold ETFs?

(*a*) They are held electronically in the demat form

(*b*) They are not very liquid as selling is difficult

(*c*) They are not traded in the stock exchanges

(*d*) All of the above.

A. (*a*)

Q. Which of the following financing options would not qualify to be a structured finance product?

(*a*) Project finance

(*b*) Asset based finance

(*c*) Bill discounting

(*d*) Securitization.

A. (*c*)

Q. Which of the following would suitably describe the practice of investing in difficult economic times for creating opportunity out of adversity?

(*a*) Future dealing

(*b*) Venture capital

(*c*) Vulture investing

(*d*) Contra investing.

A. (*c*)

Q. The Bombay Stock Exchange which started in 1875 did not have a scale to measure the highs and lows in the stock market. It came out with its stock index the sensex much later. When was the sensex introduced?

A. In 1986.

Q. The sensex in the beginning of 2013 has touched a figure of 20,000. To which base period is the base value of 100 of the index linked?

A. The base period of sensex is 1978-79.

Q. The sensex is calculated on the free float methodology since 2003. What is meant by free float market capitalization?

A. It is the proportion of total shares available for trading to the general public

Q. The Dow Jones Industrial Average index dropped 89 per cent from its peak and reached its bottom in July of which year during the Great Depression?

A. 1932.

Q. This term is very much in use to signify the amount of carbon dioxide released by an organization, industry or individual. What is this term?

A. Carbon footprints.

Q. In the context of mergers, takeovers we have come across terms like black knight, yellow knight. There is also a term known as white knight. What does it suggest?

A. It comes to the rescue of a company which is the target of a takeover by being a friendly acquirer.

Q. It is a term used in the context of mortgages where the investor buys the property but permits the seller who was facing a foreclosure to occupy the house as a tenant. What word is used to describe it?

A. Equity stripping.

Q. What would you understand from the term 'positional goods' which is a common business term?

A. Goods which are essentially scarce and whose scarcity cannot be reduced by increasing production for *e.g.*, works of art.

Q. There are government sponsored mortgage associations for promoting housing in the US like Government National Mortgage Association among others. What is the common name for this organization?

A. Ginnie Mae.

Q. It was founded in 1967 at Bangkok by countries like Thailand, Indonesia, Malaysia, Singapore and Philippines. What is the name of this group?

A. ASEAN Association of South East Asian Nations.

Q. It is a Swiss city which borders Germany and France. Important banking regulations have been formulated in this city. Which city are we talking about?

A. Basel, Switzerland.

Q. Just as Sensex is to Bombay Stock Exchange what does Athex relate to?

A. The stock index of Greece.

Q. Which individual is regarded as the first woman President of a stock exchange in India?

A. Omana Abraham of Cochin Stock Exchange.

Q. In the context of financial markets and their evolution over the years there is a well known event which took place under a banyan tree at Horniman Circle in Mumbai many centuries ago. What did it lead to?

A. The start of the Bombay Stock Exchange.

Q. Which is the largest mutual fund organization in India?

A. Unit Trust of India (UTI).

Q. Which was the world's first initial public offering that saw the issue of the world's first share certificate?

A. Dutch East India Company.

Q. Joe Dun was a London bailiff during the time of King Henry VIII. He was particularly famous for letters which were known as 'dunning letters'. What kind of letters were these?

A. Credit collection letters as Joe Dun was well known for recovering money from defaulting debtors.

Q. The Japanese central bank carries out this survey among influential Japanese companies regarding current and expected business trends and conditions for the next year. What name is given to this survey?

A. Tenkan survey.

Q. Securities and Exchange Board of India has launched a portal to enable investors to lodge and follow-up complaints they may have. What is the portal called?

A. SCORES SEBI Complaints Redressal System.

Q. Investors often specify the particular share they wish to buy and indicate the price at which it may be purchased. What is the name given to this order of the investor?

A. Limit order.

Q. The term 'blue chip' is known to indicate stocks of progressive companies. The term originates from a well known game. Which is this game?

A. Poker game.

Q. What term denotes a woman of high society and wealth whose debut becomes publicly visible and fancied?

A. Celebutante.

Q. Which was the first Indian bank to be listed on the New York Stock Exchange?

A. ICICI Bank.

Q. What is the name given to a professionally managed collective investment scheme which collects funds from a large number of investors and invests in different investment schemes and stock markets?

A. Mutual fund.

Q. Who was the first US President in office to visit the New York Stock Exchange?

A. Ronald Reagan made the first of his two visits to the NYSE while serving as US President on 28th March, 1985.

Q. The owner of the NYSE agreed in 2012 to an 8.2 billion USD deal that would give control of this longstanding symbol of American capitalism to the organization ICE. What is this organization known as?

A. Inter Continental Exchange.

Q. What is the name of Mexico's only stock exchange?

A. BOLSA.

Q. What do you understand from a company's statement when it announces that bonus shares would be issued in the ratio of 3:1?

A. The existing shareholders would get 3 bonus shares for every share held by them.

Q. India's first mortgage firm IMGC has been set-up with the association of National Housing Bank, International Finance Corporation, Asian Development Bank and US based Genworth. What is the name of this mortgage body?

A. Indian Mortgage Guarantee Company.

Q. If an investor is investing at the cut-off price in an initial public offering of a company what does it mean?

A. In such cases the investor is investing at the highest price of the price band.

Q. The movement in the prices of stocks before it really hits rock bottom is likened to a 'dead cat bounce'. What does it reflect?

A. It refers to a stock price which while crashing experiences a brief rally before coming down to hit the lowest.

Q. It is a market phenomenon where short-term contracts are less expensive than long-term contracts. What is the name given to it?

A. Contango.

Q. Brokers receive instructions from stockholders to sell a stock at a fixed price or not to sell at all. What is the term for such trading?

A. 'Fill' or 'kill' trade.

Q. Between 1870 and 1903 a gong was used at stock exchanges to signify the end of a trading session. Later a bell was introduced and is still in use for this purpose. What is the term used to identify this practice?

A. Closing bell.

Q. October 29, 1929 is reckoned as the date of the great stock market crash which led to the years of the Great Depression. How has this date come to be known as?

A. Black Tuesday.

Q. There are a class of nominal shares known as 'golden shares'. What special privilges does it provide?

A. Voting rights which can out vote all other shareholders in certain specified situations.

Q. Certain specified financial instruments are known as 'Section 54 EC' bonds which indicate the nature of benefits it carries. What is the benefit that the bondholder gets from investing in these bonds?

A. Exemption from paying long-term capital gains tax on sale of residential property.

Q. Standard & Poor Dividend Aristocrats and S&P High Yield Dividend Aristocrat are two indices which track the performances of companies which have continuously paid dividends over a period of 25 years. What is the special attribute of these companies that it tracks?

A. The continuous increase in the amount of dividends it pays.

Q. A subsection of the London Stock Exchange is called AIM. It was launched in 1995 with the aim of allowing smaller companies to sell their shares to the public. What is the name of this subsection?

A. Alternative Investment Market.

Q. What is the strategy used by traders to sell when they anticipate a fall in the stock prices?

A. Short sell.

Q. What is the situation known as in which an entrepreneur starts a company with little capital which is mainly from personal finances and then grows with the funds generated from operating revenues?

A. Bootstrapping.

Q. Where in the world would you find the largest diamond bourse which was recently inaugurated?

A. Mumbai.

Q. About which famous personality G D Birla is reported to have said 'He has a lot of money but is he happy'?

A. J R D Tata.

Q. Hawala transactions are prohibited under the provisions of which Act in India?

A. Foreign Exchange Management Act (FEMA).

Q. A new share index on environment sustainable stocks has been launched at the Bombay Stock Exchange. What is the name of this index?

A. BSE Greenex.

Q. It is a stock market index of over 6,000 world stocks. It is maintained by the company which was formerly Morgan Stanley Capital International and is often used as a common benchmark for global stock funds. Name this index?

A. MSCI World Index.

Q. This stock index represents large, medium and small cap companies across 18 countries of Europe. It has a fixed number of 600 components. Can you identify this index?

A. STOXX Europe 600.

Q. He is the founder of Nomura Securities which is commonly known as the 'Gulliver' in Japan. Who is he?

A. Tokushichi Nomura II.

Q. The Toronto Index Participation Fund TIP 35 was launched in 1935 and has the distinction of being the first in the world in its category. Which is this category?

A. It was the world's first exchange traded fund.

Q. When was the first Economic Survey presented for India? It has since become a yearly review of the economy by the government.

A. It was presented for the first time for the financial year 1951-52

Q. Reserve Bank of India often refers to Open Market Operations as part of its responsibilities. Which specific area of responsibility does it mean?

A. The management of credit policy.

Q. The Bombay Stock Exchange has started its first thematic carbon based index BSE Carbonex which is modelled on the UK's FTSE CDP index. What is this index meant to track?

A. The companies' commitment to climate change mitigation by creating a benchmark and awareness about the risks posed by climate change.

Q. We often hear about companies disclosing receipt of ISO 9000 certification. What does ISO 9000 certificate indicate?

A. These are quality standards developed by International Standards Organization in Geneva that requires companies to document their commitment to quality at all levels of their organization.

Q. Brokers and subbrokers are required to be registered with Securities and Exchange Board of India to be able to trade in the stock markets. How is the investor supposed to differentiate between a broker and subbroker while dealing with them?

A. The registration number of a broker starts with letters 'INB' while that of a subbroker begins with 'INS'.

Q. Issuers of initial public offers are required to file their prospectus with SEBI detailing the terms and conditions of their offer. In this context what is a shelf-prospectus?

A. This prospectus enables an issuer to make a series of issues within a period of one year without the need of filing a fresh prospectus every time.

Q. This special facility of shelf-prospectus is not available to all issuers of public issues. Which particular category of companies is eligible for this facility?

A. Public sector banks/financial institutions.

Q. Pricing of public issues is not controlled by the regulatory authority in India. When did the Indian primary market usher in an era of free pricing?

A. In 1992.

Q. The pricing of public issues is decided by the issuer in consultation with the merchant banker on the basis of market demand. Which are the two methods of pricing that are adopted by the issuer?

A. The Fixed Price mechanism and the Book Building method.

Q. Stock lending and borrowing systems enable traders to short sell stocks in the market. What does this system operate?

A. In this system traders borrow shares that they do not possess or lend those shares which they own but do not intend to sell immediately.

Q. Indian Depository Receipts IDRs have emerged as a form of raising funds by corporates. What is this instrument?

A. An IDR is a depository receipt denominated in Indian rupees and issued by a depository in India. It represents ownership in a fixed number of shares.

Q. There is an international index which tracks the world's 100 wealthiest individuals daily. According to its ranking Carlos Slim, the Mexican telecom giant continues to be the first among the wealthiest. Which is this index?

A. Bloomberg Billionaires index.

Q. Carlos Slim who retains his position as the No.1 in the list of the world's wealthiest as of 2012 controls the largest mobile phone operator in entire America. Which is this company which is in Mexico?

A. America Movil (AMX) SAB.

Q. Traders generally mistakenly assume a stocks temporary price as its low point. What term is used to describe this practice?

A. False bottom.

Q. In 2000 this Indian banking institution was the first bank to be listed on the New York Stock Exchange with its issue of 5 million American Depository Receipts. Which was this bank?

A. ICICI Bank.

Q. Amsterdam Stock Exchange is the main stock exchange in the Netherlands and the oldest in the world. Which acronym defines this exchange?

A. AEX.

Q. There are two stock exchanges based in New York, one of which is the New York Stock Exchange. Which is the other stock exchange?

A. American Stock Exchange which is the smaller of the two exchanges.

Q. The American Stock Exchange is known as the Curb Exchange or Little Board. By what alternate name is the New York Stock Exchange known as?

A. Big Board.

Q. The national stock exchange of Australia is made up of the six exchanges in the cities of Adelaide, Brisbane, Hobart, Melbourne, Perth and Sydney. What is this national stock exchange known as?

A. Australian Stock Exchange.

Q. We have a system where securities are bought, sold and matched automatically by computers. What name is given to these trading systems?

A. Automated Screen Trading.

Q. In the US, bonds are available in small denominations of usually $ 100 which the small investors can afford to buy. There is a special name for these instruments. Can you name it?

A. Baby Bonds.

Q. The telegraph invented in 1844 paved the way for this particular machine which was invented by Edward Calahan to receive and print the latest price quotes at brokerage houses. Which is this machine used in stock exchanges that we are referring to?

A. Stock ticker machine.

Q. The Buttonwood Agreement signed in 1792 under a buttonwood tree in Wall Street led to the founding of the New York Stock Exchange. Who signed this document agreeing to what terms?

A. 24 brokers agreed to trade securities on a commission basis.

Q. The first major collapse of the US stock market happened on 24th September, 1869. Since then a special term has been coined to mean a sudden market collapse which identifies with this day. Which is this term?

A. Black Friday.

Q. These are ordinary shares with special voting rights. These shares are often owned by the founder of a company and his family. How are these shares specified?

A. B shares.

Q. It is the French word for stock exchanges and is generally used to describe European stock exchanges. Which is this word?

A. Bourse.

Q. CAC 40 is an index of prices based on the prices of 40 leading stocks. With which stock exchange is this index linked?

A. Paris Stock Exchange.

Q. A bond which can be redeemed even before it matures for payment has a special term to identify it. Which is this term?

A. Callable bond.

Q. Consols were very useful as financial instruments to fund the wars of England. What is the striking feature of these bonds?

A. These are government bonds which pay interest but do not have a maturity date.

Q. There is a class of bonds which have similar characteristics as a consol. Which are these bonds?

A. Perpetual bonds.

Q. Based on the NASDAQ model there is an European stock market which is based in Brussels and London. It is a fully regulated stock market for high growth companies with international development plans. Which stock exchange are we referring to?

A. EASDAQ.

Q. If it is said that EIBOR is a interbank offered rate most commonly used by borrowers and lenders to conduct financial transactions in a particular financial market, then which is this market that we are meaning?

A. Dubai and the surrounding Emirates.

Q. The FTSE 100 lists the top 100 companies in the London Stock Exchange. It is managed by the FTSE group. Who owns the FTSE group?

A. The FTSE group is owned by the *Financial Times* and London Stock Exchange.

Q. The HEX index is the index of stock prices on the main stock exchange in Finland. Name this stock exchange?

A. The Helsinki Stock Exchange.

Q. There is a theoretical model which is used to describe the movements of the stock markets which reflect the fashionable lengths of women's skirts. The shorter the skirt the more bullish the market is supposed to be. Which is this theory?

A. The Hemline theory.

Q. Official meetings of groups, associations, federations invariably stipulate a minimum number of members to be present to be considered as a valid meeting. This number is known as a quorum. What if there are not enough members to constitute a quorum for a meeting. What would such a meeting be called?

A. Inquorate.

Q. Which type of company would you classify as an overcapitalized company?

A. A company that has more capital than it actually needs.

Q. We are talking of a class of preference shares which are to be bought back by the company on an agreed date and for an agreed amount. How are such preference shares classified?

A. Redeemable preference shares.

Q. In the context of stock market terminology which event is known as the 'South Sea Bubble'?

A. It refers to a scandal on the London Stock Exchange linked to the collapse of the South Sea Company in 1720 when many investors lost their money.

Q. It is the oldest stock market index which tracks the performance of 30 of the largest and widely traded stocks. Which is this index?

A. Dow Jones Industrial Average.

Q. The Securities and Exchange Commission is the regulator for the securities market in USA. The companies are required to e-file their returns with the regulator. What is this e-filing system known as?

A. Electronic data gathering analysis and retrieval system.

Q. What is the term used for a trader who rapidly buys and sells stocks throughout the day?

A. Day trader.

Q. For a buyer interested in acquiring a company knowing the enterprise value is important. What factors are considered in determining the enterprise value of a company?

A. It indicates the cost of buying a company and hence takes into account the market capitalization, the debt on the company's books and the cash available on the balance sheet.

Q. The wholesale price index WPI is the most widely watched gauge of prices in India, tracking commodity prices at the wholesale level. What are the components of this price index?

A. The three major components are primary goods, fuel and power index and manufactured goods.

Q. The SARFAESI Act enables banks to recover their dues from defaulting borrowers without the intervention of courts. However, the provisions of the Act are not applicable to all loans. Which of the loans are not covered by this Act?

A. Loans below ₹ 1 lakh and where the outstanding with the bank is less than 20 per cent of the principal and interest are excluded.

Q. Companies wanting to raise funds from its existing shareholders do it through a letter offering new shares to them. What is this kind of issue called?

A. Rights issue.

Q. Each financial security carries an ISIN number which is a 12-digit alpha numeric number. What is this ISIN number?

A. International Securities Identification Number.

Q. Deep discount bonds are long-term investment options generally issued by public sector bodies. What is the special feature of these bonds?

A. The interest paid on these bonds is the difference between the face value and the issue price.

Q. Stock split and reverse stock split are two different options taken by companies to control the number of shares and their value without disturbing the total value of the existing stocks. What is the difference between the two options?

A. In a stock split the existing shares are split creating more number of shares with share of each value dropping while in the reverse split the number of existing shares is reduced to have less number of shares at higher value per share.

Q. Various unethical practices are surfacing in the stocks market which are hurting the interests of investors. Front running is one such undesirable tendency. What is its drawback?

A. It suggests involvement of employees of investment funds and brokers in trading of stocks before executing the orders of their clients to exploit the market as they are in the know of certain inside information.

Q. Which market index represents the largest companies on the Toronto Stock Exchange?

A. TSX Composite.

Q. In USA the Securities and Exchange Commission is the regulator for the stock markets. It was established after a major financial crisis in the US. What was the event and when was it established?

A. After the Great Depression in 1933.

Q. It is the largest market index which actually includes 6,500 stocks and measures the performance of all US headquartered equity securities. Which is this index?

A. Wilshire 5000.

Q. What do the letters in FTSE 100 index stand for?

A. *Financial Times* Stock Exchange.

Q. It is rather amusing but what was the reason the NASDAQ Stock Exchange was totally disabled for the day in December 1987?

A. It was due to a squirrel burroughing through a telephone line.

Q. Big institutional investors and prominent stock traders use this trading tool to get the best possible price for their stocks. This model is used by software programmers for complex trading problems. What is this form of trading known as?

A. Algorithm trading.

Q. This is a method often employed to launder the proceeds of fraud schemes by criminals who gain illegal access to deposit accounts by recruiting third parties. These third parties are sometimes not in any way connected with the schemes but are used to transfer these funds. These third parties are known by a special term. What is it?

A. Money mules.

Q. Inexperienced investors and senior citizens fall prey to petition mills and lose their savings. What is a petition mill?

A. It is a fraud in which the perpetrator acts as a financial advisor to their victims by promising them settlements of their financial crisis. They pocket money in the form of professional fees without any tangible gain to the victims.

Q. Which area in a stock exchange is defined as a 'pit'?

A. It is the area demarcated for trades transacted by the traders.

Q. Poison Pill is a defence mechanism adopted by companies when there is threat of their takeover. How does this mechanism work?

A. The target company tries to make its shares as unattractive as possible to the acquiring company.

Q. The Glass Steagall Act was passed in 1933 in the wake of financial crisis during the Great Depression. It has however been repealed in 1999. What law did this Act pass?

A. It separated investment banking from commercial banking activities.

Q. Companies use this method to inflate their sales figures before a reporting period. They do so by shipping goods to customers even though the customers may not have placed orders for it. What is this method called?

A. Trade stuffing.

Q. The term for this index was coined by James Turk in the mid-1980s which measures the percentage of stock of gold in a country's central bank divided by the quantity of that country's currency outstanding. What is the term for this index?

A. Fear index.

Q. By this process the bondholders become shareholders of a bankrupt company thereby sparing the redemptions to them. What is this process called?

A. Ball in.

Q. The constituents of this index, *viz.,* deposits, credit and investments of scheduled commercial banks are proxies for liquidity risk, credit risk and interest rate risk which are the three major risks faced by any scheduled bank in India. What is this important index known as?

A. The Banking Sector Soundness BSS index.

Q. FANGs are financial instruments issued by the federal agencies of the US government. These securities are not always guaranteed by the Treasury, hence the use of this term. What is the full form of this term?

A. Federal Agency Non Guaranteeds.

Q. In the context of subprime loans which were largely responsible for the financial crisis in the US in 2008, the term NINJA is used for these loans. What does this term denote?

A. No Income No Job and Assets loan accounts.

Q. It is a financing arrangement similar to hypothecation, the only difference being that the owner of a ship uses it as collateral. The owner continues to earn an income from the ship as it remains in his possession despite being a collateral security for the borrowing. What is the term used for this special type of financing?

A. Bottomry.

Q. Bulldog bonds are known to be sterling denominated bonds issued by non-British institutions in UK. Why is the name bulldog given to these bonds?

A. Bulldog is considered as a national symbol of England.

Q. Treasury Inflation Protected Securities (TIPS) in the US are considered as a dynamic investment as it is linked to inflation. What impact does it have on the value of the bonds and its return?

A. The face value of the bond is adjusted in line with inflation and therefore the interest which is based on the face value is also flexible.

Q. In the credit card business which type of customer payments is described as a revolver?

A. A person who makes payment on his card incrementally.

Q. These financial instruments refer to a class of mutual fund units which have a comparatively high minimum initial investment requirement. It effectively dissuades small investors from participating and is primarily targeted towards large institutional investors. It has the benefits of limited or no load charges and fees. Can you identify this class of investments?

A. Y shares.

Q. The term is meant to distinguish an acquirer company, which initially was making a takeover bid, but relented to discussing a merger with the target company. Which is this term?

A. Yellow Knight.

Q. Classifying them as Z group securities is for the information of all concerned about the status of these companies. It is intended to sound a cautionary signal to the investors. What message does it convey?

A. Z group securities are linked to companies which have not complied with all the formalities of the stock exchange. They could also be companies which have not attended to investor complaints.

Q. It is the penalty payable by a seller to the buyer in a stocks transaction for his inability to deliver the share certificate to the buyer on the settlement date. What is the term used to describe this practice?

A. Ulta badla.

Q. These funds generally identify distressed assets for investment at cheap rates and look for gains when the position improves. Many countries which are in financially weak positions are often the target of these funds. Which word aptly sums up such funds?

A. Vulture fund.

Q. You have invested in a bond instrument which informs that it would not make payment of interest during its entire tenure. The total payment is offered on maturity when the bond may also have the benefit of appreciation of its value. Can you name the type of bonds you have chosen for investing?

A. Zero coupon bond.

Q. Dividends are declared by companies based on their financial performances/results. The dividends at times remain unclaimed even after considerable length of time. What happens to such amounts?

A. These dividend amounts are transferred to Investors Education and Protection Fund.

Q. The term coined by Peter Lynch, who is considered to be one of the greatest investors of his time, is used in his book 'One up on Wall Street' to describe a stock whose value increases ten times of its purchase price. His examples of such stocks were blue chip stocks of General Electric, Hewlett Packard. Which is this term?

A. Ten bagger.

Q. An investor holding paper securities of a well known company wishes to sell the shares in the stock market. He is unable to do so. What would you suggest to him?

A. To open a demat account and credit the shares to this account after dematerialization.

Q. Just like banks have to maintain a stipulated capital adequacy ratio similarly nonbanking finance companies NBFCs are also required to do so. What is the minimum stipulation for NBFCs?

A. 15 per cent.

Q. Initial public offers are floated at a price as decided by the company either through the fixed price route or the book-building process. How is the pricing finalized in the fixed price route?

A. The share in this case is offered at a fixed price which is disclosed to the prospective investor.

Q. In the case of the book building option at what price are the shares offered?

A. The shares are offered within a price band within which the investors have to bid. The final price is decided depending upon the response from the public.

Q. It is considered to be the second largest stock exchange in the world by market value. It lists 2,500 domestic companies and 31 foreign companies. Name this exchange which is in an Asian country?

A. Tokyo Stock Exchange.

Q. What would you call a yen denominated bond which is issued in Japan by a foreign investor?

A. Samurai bond.

Q. It is the rate of interest at which banks in Asia lend funds to each other. This rate is used as a standard for other loans. We are referring to which rate?

A. Singapore Inter Bank Offered Rate (SIBOR).

Q. It is regarded as Asia's most internationalized stock exchange. It has more than 40 per cent of its listed companies from outside its country of location and is the world's biggest offshore market for Asian equity in China, India and Japan. Similarly, it is known as the Asian gateway for Asian investors to invest in global capital. Which exchange are we discussing?

A. Singapore Exchange SGX.

Q. It is a form of gambling by rogue traders by engaging in speculative deals which are unauthorized by the company. Former trader Kweku Adoboli was accused of this form of gambling while working at banking giant UBS. What is this type of gambling known as?

A. Spread betting.

Q. These financial markets have their origin in the regular meetings, usually in a restaurant, of a few men who acted as intermediaries between buyers and sellers for earning money in the form of commission. What did this form of meeting evolve into?

A. Stock exchange.

Q. In the United States a group of brokers used to meet everyday underneath a buttonwood tree on Wall Street which ultimately came to be regarded as the origin of the New York Stock Exchange, the first stock exchange in the US. What is the significance of these brokers?

A. They are recognized as the first 24 members of the New York Stock Exchange.

Q. It is a market index of Russell 3,000 and tracks the 1,000 stocks with the largest market capitalization. What is it called?

A. Russell 1000 index.

Q. This stock index is published by Frank Russell Co., Washington which tracks the stocks of 2,000 small American companies with an average market capitalization of USD 255 million. It is considered the benchmark index for small capital investments. Which is this index?

A. Russell 2000 index.

Q. The introduction of technology has impacted this traditional method adopted on the trading floor of stock exchanges by traders to strike deals by shouting out the prices at one another. This is a fairly old system which ensured a fair pricing model. What is this system called?

A. Open outcry.

Q. National Electronic Trading NEAT is a weekly settlement system where squaring up of the transactions is permitted. It is a computerized system for the capital market segment. With which institution or stock exchange is it linked?

A. It is the online trading facility of the National Stock Exchange.

Q. Mibtel denotes the index of stock prices on a prominent stock exchange in Italy. Which is this stock exchange?

A. Milan.

Q. These are shares owned by the promoter, or his family, of a company which carry special voting rights. These shares otherwise continue to be ordinary stocks. How are these shares classified as?

A. B shares.

Q. Bellwether is a term commonly used by people connected with the stock markets. It has to do with stocks which are generally of a prominent company in their respective sectors. What particular information does it convey?

A. It is a particular share or bond which is closely tracked on the stock exchanges as it is presumed to be an indicator of the market trends.

Q. What is the name given to the practice of dating a document before the date on which it is drawn up?

A. Ante date.

Q. We are referring to the European derivative exchange which started in 1998 and is located in Germany. It deals primarily with European based derivatives, facilitating trade and settlement of contracts. As a fully electronic network it is regarded as one of the most innovative electronic markets in the world. Which is this derivative exchange?

A. Eurex.

Q. If you were to buy stocks ex bonus what would you understand?

A. It means that the bonus announced by the company is for the seller of the shares and not for the buyer.

Q. FIBOR is the rate for transactions on an European money market. Which market in Europe are we referring to?

A. Frankfurt Inter Bank Offered Rate.

Q. Considered short-term securities these include debt and equity instruments that are retained for short periods of time, purchased with the intention of profiting from short-term price changes. Accounting principles require that such investments are appropriately classified and shown in the financial statements. Which class of securities are we referring to?

A. Held for trading securities.

Q. Hemline theory in stock market parlance tends to link the movements of the stock markets with the hemlines or the lengths of women's skirts. The shorter the length of the skirt the more ....the market seems to behave. What word would you use to fill in the blank?

A. Bullish.

Q. This term is attributed to the efforts of the then Chairman of the US Federal Reserve Board Alan Greenspan to prevent a down swing in the stock markets. In 1998 the Federal Reserve had lowered the interest rates following the collapse of a well known investment bank. This stimulated demand for stocks in the market as the investors could borrow funds at cheap rates. Can you name the term?

A. Greenspan put.

■■■

Institutions: Character and Features

Q. The selection of the President of the World Bank since its establishment has had one striking feature. Which is this aspect?

A. The President has always been from the United States of America.

Q. Which country was the beneficiary of the World Bank's first loan of US $ 250 million in 1947?

A. France received it for post-war reconstruction.

Q. Which bank is nick named as 'Soc Gen' which has developed as one of the biggest banks in the world?

A. Societe Generale.

Q. If Habib Bank of Pakistan is mentioned as Habib Bank AG Zurich what does it indicate?

A. AG in German means Company Limited and so it would mean Habib Bank Ltd., Zurich, Switzerland.

Q. The headquarters of the Deutsche Bank in Frankfurt has two towers named 'Soll' and 'Haber' in German. The names of these towers suggest the basic banking terms. What are these terms in English?

A. Debit and Credit.

Q. Which American institution in London was regarded as a legend during World War II when it opened for business one day after being bombed? Throughout the war it made travel and freight forwarding arrangements for Allied military personnel and diplomats.

A. American Express.

Q. 'Bank on Bike' is a novel delivery mechanism adopted by a public sector bank in India to cover the rural markets. Which is this bank?

A. State Bank of India.

Q. The largest ever merger in global financial industry was valued at US $ 91 billion recently. Which bank was acquired by which institution?

A. Barclays Bank bought ABN-Amro for this amount in 2007.

Q. In the logo of which Indian public sector bank would you find the picture of Hindu Goddess Lakshmi?

A. Dena Bank.

Q. Regional rural banks are working to promote the rural sector in India. Which are the states where the regional rural banks are not present?

A. Sikkim and Goa.

Q. Which was the first private sector bank to be established when the setting up of private banks was permitted by Reserve Bank of India?

A. Global Trust Bank.

Q. Which bank in India has the distinction of starting the first 'talking' ATM for the visually impaired?

A. Union Bank of India.

Q. It is a London based East European bank meant for supporting the economic transition in the former Eastern bloc countries and Soviet republics. This development bank is functioning for the last two decades. Which is this financial institution?

A. European Bank for Reconstruction and Development (EBRD).

Q. An international bank had one of its first overseas branch in an Indian city. It has recently celebrated 200 years of its existence in India. Which is this bank?

A. Citi Bank.

Q. Which are the only two public sector banks to have merged so far in the Indian banking sector?

A. Punjab National Bank and New Bank of India in 1993.

Q. The development financial institution ICICI Ltd., merged with ICICI Bank to form the financial conglomerate. What was the full form of ICICI Ltd., when it started as the development financial institution?

A. Industrial Credit and Investment Corporation of India Ltd.

Q. This bank traces its history to 1904 when Amadeo Giannini founded the Bank of Italy in San Francisco for the benefit of the immigrants who were deprived of banking services. Which bank are we talking about?

A. Bank of America.

Q. This bank which recently merged was itself founded from the merger of Algemene Bank Nederland and Amsterdamsche and Rotterdamsche Bank. Identify this bank?

A. ABN-Amro Bank.

Q. This central bank was founded in 1694, nationalized in 1946 and gained independence in 1997. Identify this institution?

A. Bank of England.

Q. This public sector bank offers an unusual service for the pilgrims at the Tirupati temple. Name this bank?

A. Bank of Baroda.

Q. An Irish playwright Paul Howard has created a musical satire 'Anglo' which recounts through songs and drama how a prominent Irish bank fuelled the property boom and then collapsed costing the Irish tax payer up to 20 billion euros so far. Which is this bank?

A. Anglo Irish Bank.

Q. With which mutual fund would you link this following commercial line 'You have made three kinds of investments: (*i*) fixed deposits (*ii*) fixed deposits (*iii*) fixed deposits'?

A. Franklin Templeton Investments.

Q. This financial institution has its headquarters named as 'Yogakshema' derived from the Rig Veda. Which is this institution?

A. Life Insurance Corporation of India.

Q. Pakistan's Habib Bank currently has its headquarters in Karachi. It however started from a different place in 1941. What was its first location?

A. Bombay now Mumbai.

Q. Banks carry distinctive logos which identify them. Which bank has a spread eagle as its logo?

A. Barclays Bank.

Q. The HDFC Bank network has branches of two other banks which merged with it as a single entity. Which are these two banks which had earlier merged among themselves?

A. Centurion Bank and Bank of Punjab.

Q. This bank is generally perceived to be the first to start credit card business in India. Which is this bank that we are referring to?

A. Andhra Bank.

Q. An Indian public sector bank has opened the first lockless branch in a small village Shani Shingnapure in Maharashtra. Which is this bank?

A. UCO Bank.

Q. The Catholic church in Kerala mobilized funds approximating ₹ 250 crore from its non-resident supporters for acquiring a stake in this bank. It however gave up this holding later in 2010. Can you identify the bank?

A. Catholic Syrian Bank.

Q. The website of the European Central Bank sports 'Economia'. What is it?

A. A game that teaches the basics of the European Union monetary policy.

Q. Floating rate of interest on deposits is a new offering from banks in India. Which private sector recently launched floating rate deposit scheme?

A. IDBI Bank.

Q. Till recently Reserve Bank of India was the major shareholder in State Bank of India. Which authority has taken over the shares of RBI?

A. Government of India.

Q. Federal Deposit Insurance Corporation was established to insure deposits in commercial banks in USA. What event prompted the setting up of this institution?

A. When commercial banks failed in the USA during the Great Depression of 1929-33.

Q. There is an international body of securities regulators and standard setters. The members of this global policy forum regulate more than 95 per cent of the world's securities market in 115 jurisdictions. Which is this international body?

A. International Organization of Securities Commissions (IOSCO).

Q. The small savings schemes are operated through the country wide network of post offices in India. Which organization is authorized by the Government of India to manage these funds?

A. National Small Savings Fund (NSSF).

Q. The London Inter Bank Offered Rate LIBOR which is caught in a huge controversy is set daily after the designated banks provide their borrowing costs to a central authority. Which is this authority?

A. British Bankers' Association.

Q. Banks are thinking of many innovative ways to reach out to their customers. One such effort is the bank branch aboard a boat on the river Amazon. It is considered to be the world's first floating bank branch. Which is the bank and where is it?

A. It is Brazil's Banco Bradesco.

Q. There is this bank in Vatican City whose chief executive reports directly to a committee of cardinals and ultimately to the Pope. It was founded in 1942 and is commonly known as the Vatican Bank. What is the other name for this bank?

A. The Institute for Works of Religion.

Q. There is a body in India which was founded in 1958 with a mandate to lay down the terms and conditions for compliance by the authorized dealers in foreign exchange. Which agency are we referring to?

A. Foreign Exchange Dealers' Association of India (FEDAI).

Q. AXIS Bank is one of the top three private sector banks in India. By what name was it known earlier?

A. UTI Bank.

Q. What is common to the three banks Canara Bank, Karnataka Bank and Vijaya Bank?

A. All three banks started from Mangalore.

Q. Grindlays Bank was a well known foreign bank operating in India before it stopped functioning. Which Indian bank had acquired the Shimla and Darjeeling branches of Grindlays Bank in 2002?

A. ICICI Bank.

Q. Two aircrafts of an Indian private airline have been taken into possession by one of the world's largest aircraft financier. The bank has also filed a case against the civil aviation regulator in India for delaying deregistration of the aircrafts. Which is this bank?

A. DVB Bank of Germany.

Q. India has become a full fledged member of the Financial Action Task Force. India became the 34th member of this inter governmental body. What is the role of this body?

A. It is responsible for setting global standards on antimoney laundering and combating the financing of terrorism.

Q. Which was India's first depository to start functioning in 1996 that ensured that securities were held in paperless dematerialized format?

A. National Securities Depository Ltd.

Q. In 1913 Rabindranath Tagore became the first non-European to win the Nobel Prize for Literature. The prize cheque was drawn on which bank?

A. British Grindlays Bank.

Q. Which foreign bank held a 30 per cent stake in Allahabad Bank Ltd., before its nationalization?

A. Standard Chartered Bank.

Q. The Parliament passed the Banking Companies (Acquisition and Transfer of Undertakings) Act in August 1969. What was achieved by approving this bill?

A. Nationalization of the largest 14 commercial Indian banks.

Q. The concept of reverse mortgage loans for the senior citizens in India was introduced sometime in India by a private financial company. Which was the first commercial bank to offer such loans to senior citizens in India and when?

A. State Bank of India started the scheme in October 2007.

Q. It is an independent and autonomous body set-up with the collaborative efforts of the Reserve Bank of India and banks. It acts as a watchdog to monitor and to ensure that the banking practices adopted by member banks are adhered to while delivering the services as promised to customers. Identify this important authority?

A. Banking Codes and Standards Board of India.

Q. The bank was regarded as a success story of a professional entrepreneur. It however had to merge with a public sector bank Oriental Bank of Commerce amid allegations of insider trading and a growing portfolio of bad loans. Which was this bank?

A. Global Trust Bank.

Q. This bank with its registered office in Gangtok and headquarters in Kolkata was alleged to be a laundering machine for a few politicians from the southern states. The major share holder was a leading Kolkata based stock broker whose good days came to an end in 2001. After RBI inspection it was decided to merge this bank with Bank of Baroda. Which bank are we referring to?

A. Sikkim Bank.

Q. Investigations into the working of Bank of Rajasthan revealed a unusual shareholding structure where small, insignificant individuals were holding shares worth crore while fronting for large shareholders. It was decided to merge Bank of Rajasthan with a leading Indian bank. Which bank took over Bank of Rajasthan?

A. ICICI Bank.

Q. Industrial Development Bank of India was carved out of RBI in 1964 as a subsidiary to finance the industrial development in the country. As a financial subsidiary it did exceedingly well and within a decade fulfilled the role of a development finance company. It however underwent a major transformation in 1976. What was this change?

A. It was delinked from RBI in 1976 and was declared an autonomous financial institution.

Q. CERSAI has been promoted by the Central Government as a fraud prevention agency. It became operational in March 2011 and is considered an important addition to check malpractices in lending by banks. What is the role of this agency?

A. CERSAI or Central Electronic Registry of Securitisation Asset Reconstruction and Security Interest of India is the agency with which the borrower has to compulsorily register the title deeds of a transaction involving immovable property. In this way multiple lending on the same immovable property would be avoided.

Q. The setting up of the Financial Stability Development Council by the government created much debate and controversy in the financial sector. Which authority was selected to head this Council?

A. The Minister of Finance.

Q. This is an apex institution which was set-up in 1982 to finance the foreign trade of the country. It was given the responsibility to handle the operations of the international finance wing of IDBI. Which is this organization?

A. EXIM Bank.

Q. It is a wholly-owned Government of India undertaking providing a range of credit risk insurance covers to exporters against loss in export of goods and services. In its present form it is in operation since 1983. Can you name the organization?

A. Export Credit Guarantee Corporation (ECGC).

Q. Wegelin & Co., Switzerland's oldest private bank may pay as much as US $ 74 million after pleading guilty to US authorities for illegally helping American citizens. What is the offence the bank is accused of?

A. It assisted US tax payers in hiding assets from the US Internal Revenue Service.

Q. This well known private sector bank started its activities from Laxmi Vilas Palace, a famous landmark of Baroda. It recently acquired a small bank after overcoming stiff resistance from the employees of the target bank. Which bank are we referring to?

A. ICICI Bank.

Q. The history of Standard Chartered Bank reveals that it got its name from two banks after their merger in 1969. Which are these two banks?

A. Chartered Bank of India, Australia and China and Standard Bank of British South Africa.

Q. This institution was established under an Act of Parliament in April 1990 as the primary financial institution for financing the promotion and development of the small-scale sector which now includes the micro sector as well. Which bank are we referring to?

A. Small Industries Development Bank of India.

Q. Which legislation in the early 1900s facilitated the start of the cooperative banks in India?

A. The Cooperative Credit Societies Act, 1904.

Q. It was started in 1973 as a cooperative of US and European banks and is used as a network for transmitting financial messages and international payments. It became operational from 1976 and is in its second stage of development. Which is this organization?

A. Society for Worldwide Interbank Financial Telecommunication (SWIFT).

Q. The Indian budget of 1996-97 had announced an important policy measure regarding the development of commercial banking in India. It was meant to address the problems of the rural areas which were persisting despite regional rural banks and cooperative banks. What was it about?

A. The setting up of local area banks.

Q. These banks in India were formerly known as the Exchange banks as they were the only ones transacting most of the import and export financing business in the country. Which are these banks?

A. The foreign banks operating in India.

Q. The banking sector in India comprises of the scheduled banks and the nonscheduled banks. How would you define a nonscheduled bank?

A. Those banks which are not included in the Second schedule of the RBI Act are termed as nonscheduled banks. Their paid-up capital and reserves do not aggregate to more than ₹ 5 lakh.

Q. It is an old private sector bank having started in 1930. In 2002 the management of this bank was taken over by a foreign bank. Which is this well known bank we are talking about?

A. ING Vysya Bank.

Q. ABN-Amro was found guilty of fund transfers to Libya and Iran through New York. It was fined US$ 500 million in 2007. It however did not pay the fine amount. Why?

A. The fine was settled by Royal Bank of Scotland which had acquired ABN-Amro by then.

Q. Basel Committee on Banking Supervision is a forum for discussions on the handling of specific supervisory problems of central banks among national authorities. What is the composition of this committee?

A. It is a committee of central bank supervisors consisting of members from each of the G 10 countries.

Q. This international organization was established in 1930 and is based in Basel, Switzerland. It facilitates central banks to coordinate in a group on a wide range of policy matters and provides certain financial facilities to them. Which is this important international institution?

A. Bank for International Settlements (BIS).

Q. Which central bank in the world is celebrating 100 years of its existence in 2013?

A. US Federal Reserve.

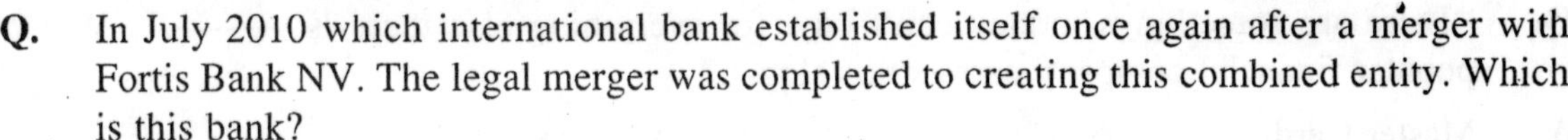

Q. In July 2010 which international bank established itself once again after a merger with Fortis Bank NV. The legal merger was completed to creating this combined entity. Which is this bank?

A. ABN-Amro Bank NV.

Q. A public sector bank is promoting 24x7 bank branches for wealthy Indians and non-resident Indians. Branches which would cater to about 40 to 50 customers are being promoted under the 'Kohinoor' brand. Which is this bank?

A. State Bank of India and its associates of the State Bank group.

Q. The position of the Chairman of the Asian Development Bank is invariably allotted to a person belonging to which country?

A. Japan.

Q. Nonbanking finance companies are considered to be suitable for getting licences for opening banks in India. Which is the first nonbanking finance company in the Indian banking history to convert to a bank?

A. Kotak Mahindra Bank.

Q. Financial institutions like the LIC, GIC, UTI, ADB and ICICI jointly established India's first credit rating agency in 1988. Name this rating agency?

A. CRISIL.

Q. In 2004 this development financial institution converted itself into a bank. In April next year, *i.e.*, 2005 it merged its banking subsidiary with itself to form one entity. Which is this bank?

A. IDBI Bank.

Q. These institutions were created by a directive of the RBI in 1987. They float deposit schemes for the general public to raise resources for business. They are not under any major regulatory constraint except that the deposits mobilized by them are to be invested in government bonds and other securities with ratings of high safety and above. How are these institutions known?

A. Residuary Nonbanking finance companies.

Q. This institution provides exclusive clearing and settlement of transactions in the money, government securities and forex markets in India. Which institution is being referred to?

A. Clearing Corporation of India Ltd. (CCIL).

Q. Under this financial programme the US Treasury injected substantial funds in nine major US banks like Bank of America, Citi group, JP Morgan Chase, Wells Fargo, etc., to protect them from the effects of the subprime crisis in 2008. What was the name given to this programme?

A. Troubled Asset Relief Program (TARP).

Q. The first urban cooperative credit society was registered in 1904 in the erstwhile Madras province of India. Which was this district?

A. Canjeevaram.

Q. "There are somethings money can't buy, for everything else there is ———". Which popular financial company carries this slogan?

A. Master Card.

Q. A new division has been created in Reserve Bank of India to have close and continuous supervision of 12 large and systemically important banking groups. Please name this important division?

A. Financial Conglomerate Monitoring Division (FCMD).

Q. The Board of Financial Supervision (BFS) which is a committee of the Central Board of the Reserve Bank of India was constituted to undertake integrated supervision of the different sectors of the financial system. Which are the financial entities supervised by it?

A. These are banks, nonbanking financial companies including primary dealers and financial institutions.

Q. The Inter bank Mobile Payment System (IMPS) is a unique initiative of the Reserve Bank of India to promote mobile banking. How does this mechanism operate?

A. It is a centralized infrastructure which enables money transfer between customer accounts in different banks through mobile phones in real time.

Q. This bank which is well known for its work in the field of microfinance has opened offices in New York, America with branches in Detroit, San Francisco, Webraska. Which is this bank that is associated with Mohd Yunus of Grameen Bank?

A. Grameen America.

Q. Federal National Mortgage Association and Federal Home Mortgage Corporation are privately owned but government sponsored to promote home ownership and affordable housing in the US. Both these institutions are better known by their common names. What are these names?

A. Fannie Mae and Freddie Mac.

Q. During the 13th century these bankers from Northern Italy gradually replaced the Jews as the traditional moneylenders. The business skills of the Italians are visible by their invention of the double entry system of bookkeeping. These Italians were known by their special name. What is this name?

A. Lombards.

Q. Amsterdam stock exchange the oldest in the world merged with the Paris and Brussels stock exchange to form a new entity in 2000. Which is this new stock institution?

A. Euronext Amsterdam.

Q. It was the first municipal corporation in India to opt for a credit rating. The rating was secured from CRISIL in 1998. Which is this municipal corporation?

A. Ahmedabad Municipal Corporation.

Q. Which is the new stock exchange in India with its benchmark index the SX-40 competing with the Sensex and Nifty?

A. MCX-SX.

Q. What is the name of the central bank of China?

A. People's Bank of China.

Q. Dividends which remain unpaid after 7 years are transferred to this fund account known as the Investor Education and Protection Fund. This fund is meant to promote what particular purpose?

A. It is for spreading awareness about the working of capital markets for investor protection.

Q. The Federal Reserve System in the US is made up of different authorities each with its specific responsibilities. What role does the Federal Open Market Committee perform within this set up?

A. The Federal Open Market Committee is responsible for the monetary policy of the country.

Q. What is the name given to the Board of Governors appointed by the President of The United States to the Federal Reserve System?

A. The Federal Reserve Board.

Q. The Federal Reserve System is unique in the sense that it has more than one Federal Reserve Bank. The Federal Reserve Banks represent the different regions in the United States. How many Federal Reserve Banks are there within the system?

A. There are 12 regional Federal Reserve Banks.

Q. The Basel Committee on Banking Supervision (BCBS) has formulated a set of regulatory guidelines for strategically important banks in every country whose failure or impairment would have external effects. The purpose of this framework is to check the adverse effects from failure through better supervision, risk management and higher capital requirements. What is the nomenclature used for these banks?

A. Domestically Systematically Important Banks (D-SIB).

Q. Known as the oldest merchant bank (1762 to 1995) in London until its collapse in 1995 after one of the bank's employee lost about 1.3 billion US dollars of bank funds in speculative investing, primarily in futures contract. Which was this bank?

A. Barings Bank.

Q. Considered as a successful banking business model it offers services on mergers and acquisitions. They also arrange private equity deals for small and medium sized enterprises. These institutions with limited means as compared to big investment banks prefer to deal with caution with their clients. What is the name given to such institutions?

A. Boutique Banks.

Q. This is a multinational debit card service of the Master Card organization. It was started in 1990 to promote the use of debit cards. What name is given to this card?

A. Maestro Card.

Q. Which of the following class of banks would qualify as a scheduled bank in India?

(*i*) Nationalized banks

(*ii*) Private sector banks

(*iii*) Foreign banks

(*iv*) All of the above.

A. (*iv*)

Q. In August, 2011 a rating agency lowered the credit rating for the US government for the first time in its history. Can you name which agency did it?

(*i*) Standard & Poor

(*ii*) Fitch

(*iii*) Moody's

(*iv*) Dow Jones.

A. (*i*)

Q. The first loan given by World Bank was of US$ 250 million to a country for post-war reconstruction. Which country was the recipient of this loan?

(*i*) France

(*ii*) Germany

(*iii*) Italy

(*iv*) Japan.

A. (*i*)

Q. Which of the following is regarded as the first listed company on the New York Stock Exchange?

(*i*) DuPont

(*ii*) Wiley

(*iii*) Bank of New York

(*iv*) General Electric.

A. (*iii*)

Q. It is the first Indian bank to open a branch outside India in London in 1946. Identify the bank from the following?

(*i*) State Bank of India

(*ii*) Bank of India

(*iii*) Canara Bank

(*iv*) Central Bank of India.

A. (*ii*)

Q. The 'OASIS' report dealt with reforming which of the following sectors?

(*i*) Insurance

(*ii*) Mutual funds

(*iii*) Pension

(*iv*) Banking.

A. (*iii*)

Q. As per the Microfinance Bill 2012 which authority will regulate all the Indian microfinance companies?

(*i*) RBI

(*ii*) IRDA

(*iii*) SEBI

(*iv*) Finance Ministry.

A. (*i*)

■■■

QUIZ SEVEN

Currencies, Coins and History

Q. Issue of paper currencies is the responsibility of the Reserve Bank of India. Under which provisions of the law does RBI exercise this authority?

A. Under Section 22 of the Reserve Bank of India Act, 1934.

Q. These coins which are mostly counterfeit, are made from base metals and plated with a precious metal to look like its solid metal counterpart. How are these coins known as?

A. Fourrie, the term is also used to mean ancient silver plated coins.

Q. Reserve currency is an important element in the economy of a country. What does reserve currency represent?

A. It is the holding of foreign currency by the central bank of a country and also used in payment for foreign transactions.

Q. When was the dollar officially adopted as the US currency?

A. In 1785.

Q. Currencies often are known by local names or slangs which incidentally are commonly used. Which major international currency is known as 'green backs'?

A. The US dollar.

Q. The first European bank notes are reported to have been printed in Sweden. In what form and when were these bank notes printed?

A. These bank notes were minted in the form of copper plate in 1644.

Q. The word 'rupiya' was coined by Sher Shah Suri during his reign of India from 1540-45 to denote his currency. In what form was this currency available?

A. It was a silver coin weighing 178 grains equivalent to 11.53 grams.

Q. In 1861 the Government of India introduced paper money. The rupee was used even during the times of British India. What form did it have then?

A. It was a silver coin having 91.7 per cent silver content by weight.

Q. When paper money was first introduced in India which was the denomination of the currency?

A. The first paper money was of ₹ 10 denomination.

Q. Which is the official legend that appears on US currency coins and paper currency?

A. 'In GOD we trust'.

Q. If you were to receive a 'sen' what would it be?

A. it is one hundredth part of one yen the Japanese currency.

Q. What is the term given to Canada's one dollar coin?

A. Loonie.

Q. Paper currency and coins usually carry portraits of leaders of the respective countries. The portrait of Yousuf Bin Ishak appears on the currency notes of which country?

A. Singapore.

Q. What is the name given to the currency of Ghana?

A. Cedi.

Q. In Kautilya's Arthashastra what role did a 'rupadarshaka' perform?

A. He was the examiner of coins.

Q. If someone were to mention 'squid' for the currency of a particular country which currency would it mean?

A. British pound.

Q. Coins when minted may suffer from certain defects as part of the production process. What is the term used for such coins?

A. FIDO.

Q. The US one cent coin is made of zinc metal coated with copper. What is it commonly called?

A. Lincoln penny.

Q. You have been given 10 dimes for an odd job in the US. How many dollars is it equivalent to?

A. Since one dime means 10 cents then 10 dimes would be equal to 100 cents or 1 dollar.

Q. It is a US gold coin worth 20 dollars which was struck between 1850 and 1933. What was it known as?

A. Double eagle.

Q. India has number of mints where coins are produced. Which one of them is the oldest mint?

A. First mint at Calcutta.

Q. Which of the currencies among euro, koku, drachma signify a weight in grams?

A. Koku of Japan.

Q. In which denomination was India's first bimetallic coins issued in 2009?

A. ₹ 10 denomination.

Q. What is the name of the process which verifies the purity of gold?

A. Assay.

Q. This word if translated literally means a 'round object' or 'round coin'. During the Qing dynasty it was a round, silver coin. To which item are we referring?

A. Yuan, the Chinese currency.

Q. Besides India, the word rupee is used by other countries like Mauritius, Nepal, Pakistan, Sri Lanka for their respective currencies. Name yet another country which has the word rupee for its currency?

A. Seychelles.

Q. Bank vaults are the store house of currency across the world. Where in the world would you find the biggest bank vault?

A. Chase Manhattan bank building in New York, USA.

Q. When did Reserve Bank of India start holding its foreign currency in US dollars?

A. From 1975.

Q. After the introduction of the decimal coinage system, 3 paise coins were first introduced to reduce the demand for 2 paise and 1 paisa coins. When was the 3 paise coin introduced in India?

A. In 1964.

Q. The coins of which dynasty from among Mauryas, Guptas, Nandas, Cholas of ancient India reveal their love for music?

A. Gupta dynasty.

Q. Purity of gold is an important criteria for accepting the particular gold jewellery or bar as security for sanction of gold loans. What is meant by 22-carat gold in this context?

A. Means 22 parts are of gold and 2 parts are of impurity or other metals.

Q. What would you call a gram of jewellery which is certified as having 91.6 per cent of gold?

A. It is 22-carat gold.

Q. Denmark, Sweden, Poland are members of the European Union but have a major difference with some members like Greece, Spain and Germany. What is this difference?

A. Denmark, Sweden, Poland do not use Euro as their official currency.

Q. If you were asked to identify 'white gold' what would you mention?

A. White gold refers to an alloy of platinum and gold.

Q. Coins which are minted for a collection or presentation and are not circulated for use as currency have a special name. What is this special name?

A. Proof coins.

Q. Error coins are in great demand from coin collectors. Why are they called error coins?

A. These are coins in which minor errors had crept in during the minting process.

Q. American Gold Eagles are known to sell at a premium owing to their gold content. What are these Eagles?

A. These are US 10 dollar coins minted in 4 sizes of one ounce and less of gold.

Q. When Greece entered the Eurozone it had accepted the euro as its official currency. Which well known and ancient currency did the euro replace?

A. Drachma.

Q. A country's currency is famously inscribed with a telling line which reads as 'This is the root of all evil'. Which country are we referring to?

A. Vatican city.

Q. ISO 4217 is the international standard applicable to which particular financial product or service?

A. It is the three letter international currency code for the currency of each country like INR for Indian rupee.

Q. Name the only country which has only paper currency and no coins; it even introduced the use of cheques only in 1997?

A. Vietnam.

Q. If paise is to rupee, cents to dollar, pence to pound then what is puls to ——?

A. Afghani, the currency of Afghanistan where 100 puls equal to 1 Afghani.

Q. Indian currency carries the portrait of Mahatma Gandhi and other scenic pictures. Which denomination has the Himalayan mountains on the obverse?

A. ₹ 100 denomination notes.

Q. Euro coins show the denomination on the common side but what is shown on the reverse side?

A. The reverse side shows an image specially chosen by the country that issued the coin.

Q. The euro symbol is inspired by which Greek symbol?

A. Epsilon.

Q. They are known as alternative currencies; are decentralized digital international currencies and are most widely used digital currency with a market cap reportedly exceeding 110 million US dollars. What are we talking about?

A. Bit coins.

Q. This four letter Botswana currency replaced the rand in 1976; the word means rain in the local language of Botswana. Can you name the currency?

A. Pula.

Q. There are two Asian nations that use the US dollar as their currency. One of them is the tiny island of Palau. Which is the other country?

A. The recently independent country of East Timor.

Q. The currency of Georgia is an anagram of the Asian currency 'rial'. Can you name the currency?

A. Lari.

Q. Before adopting the euro as their currency, Turkey, Italy and the Vatican City had the same currency. Which was this currency?

A. Lira.

Q. If you buy gold jewellery marked with KDM stamp what does it indicate?

A. The gold jewellery is soldered with cadmium.

Q. Venezuala's currency is named after one of its political statesman who revolted against the Spanish rule. Can you name the currency?

A. Bolivar.

Q. There is reference to the zero rupee note which was printed in 2007. Since then more than one million pieces have been printed. What are we referring to?

A. It is simply a piece of paper of the colour of a 50 rupee note with no value which has been introduced by a non-governmental organization opposing the giving and taking of bribes.

Q. After the introduction of the decimal system in India, coins were issued in the denomination of naya paisa. The coins were subsequently known as paisa. When was the term 'naya' dropped?

A. From 1st June, 1964.

Q. It is known as the famous gold coin of Florence in Italy and was invented in 1252. What is the name of this coin?

A. Florin.

Q. Belgium celebrated the 75th anniversary in 2004 of the world famous cartoon character by having the portrait of the character with his dog on the obverse of the 10 euro coin. Which well known character are we talking about?

A. Tintin and his dog Snowy

Q. Among the 15 languages that appear on the language panel of Indian currency notes which is the language of a neighbouring country that is included in this panel?

A. Nepal.

Q. Bolivian peso is one name of the currency of Bolivia. What is the other name for this currency?

A. Boliviano.

Q. Mannat is the common currency of two of the former Soviet republics. Which are these countries?

A. Azerbaijan and Turkmenistan.

Q. How many countries in the European Union share the same currency 'euro'?

A. 17.

Q. The Latin American countries of Argentina, Chile, Columbia, Uruguay have peso as their currency. Which is the Asian country which also has peso as its currency?

A. Philippines.

Q. This currency has its trading code as IRR and was introduced in 1798. Which currency are we talking about?

A. Iranian rial.

Q. High value rial notes carry the portrait of a famous Iranian leader. Which important figure does it portray?

A. Ayatollah Khomeini.

Q. The word 'rial' besides being the name of the Iranian currency is also the name of the currency of yet another country. Which is that country?

A. Yemeni rial.

Q. When a currency trades outside its borders in a foreign market like euro trading in US markets, what would it be known as?

A. Xeno currency.

Q. The currency we are talking about is named after the Spanish explorer Balboa and is used in addition to the US dollar. Which country and currency are we mentioning?

A. Panama and Panamian Balboa.

Q. If you are in possession of 'Benjamins' which currency are you expected to be carrying?

A. 100 US dollar bills.

Q. Reserve Bank of India's Monetary Museum traces the evolution of money in India through its coinage and financial instruments. Where is this unique presentation located?

A. Phirozeshah Mehta Road in Mumbai.

Q. Hyderabad state was the only state having its own currency during British rule in India. What was the name of this currency?

A. Osmania sicca.

Q. Platinum is a precious metal, rarer and more valuable than gold. If the jewellery is marked 'platinum' what does it signify?

A. It means the jewellery contains at least 95 per cent platinum as only then it can be considered pure.

Q. While yuan is the official unit of currency of China what is the official denomination of the currency?

A. Renminbi.

Q. If we are to say that the word 'won' represents the currency of two countries then which are the countries we are referring to?

A. South Korea and North Korea.

Q. Real is the currency of one of the member countries of the BRICS group of nations. Which is this country?

A. Brazil.

Q. Most coins carry the design on the coin on a slightly raised surface. What is this raised portion known as?

A. Relief (coin).

Q. Numismatics is the hobby of collecting coins; there is a similar habit relating to the study of paper money or bank notes. What is the name given to this study?

A. Notaphily.

Q. In the US there is a practice of identifying the particular mint from which a coin has been struck. How does this practice work?

A. There is a small letter on the coin known as the mint mark which identifies the mint.

Q. Coins are made from a variety of metals like gold, silver, bronze, copper and nickel. Each coin carries two important details. Which are these?

A. The value and the year of manufacture.

Q. Ngultrum is the currency of a country which till its adoption followed the barter system. The currency was introduced only in 1974. This currency belongs to which country?

A. Bhutan.

Q. This coin is often bought as an investment; it contains one ounce of gold. Can you connect these details to identify the coin in question?

A. Kruger rand of South Africa.

Q. If you were introduced to an individual who is regarded as a keen follower of the subject of exonumia what would you understand?

A. The study of coin like objects such as tokens and medals used for commemorative purposes is exonumia.

Q. The name of this currency is derived from 'thaler' which was a pure gold coin issued by the Hapsburg administration of Austria. Which currency is being discussed?

A. US dollar.

Q. Several countries can use the same currency as in the case of euro or a country can declare the currency of another country to be legal tender as well. Which are the countries which have declared US dollar as legal tender in their respective countries?

A. Panama and El Salvador.

Q. This country replaced their existing currency sole with a new currency inti in 1985. The inti was also replaced because of its devaluation with the 'neuvo sol' in1991. Which is this country are we talking about?

A. Peru.

Q. Poland till 1924 had its currency known as marek. It had to be replaced as it had lost its value. What is the currency that replaced it and is still in use?

A. Zloty.

Q. Most US currencies and coins have the faces of their Presidents adorning them. Which president's face is on the US$ 50 bill?

A. The face of the 18th US president Ulysses S Grant is on the front with the picture of the US Capitol on the reverse side.

Q. The chronic printing of currency in this country came to an end in 2008 when the nation ran out of paper on which to print its currency. The money had become so worthless that when the country's Reserve Bank capped personal withdrawals at $ 5,00,000 they were worth a mere 25 cents in US currency. Which is this country?

A. Zimbabwe.

Q. George Washington was one of the well known US Presidents. Which US currency carried his picture?

A. US 1 dollar bill.

Q. In which of the following places South Africa, California, Iraq, Egypt did the first gold rush take place?

A. It was in 1848 that the discovery of gold in California sparked a so-called 'gold rush'.

Q. Among Dubai, London, Shanghai and Mumbai which place do you think is the epicentre of global gold bullion trading?

A. London, as UK was the first country to adopt the gold standard in 1717.

Q. The portrait of this personality has adorned the currencies of 33 countries. It is considered to be the maximum for any person. Which personality are we talking about?

A. Queen Elizabeth of England.

Q. In 1903-04 coins in India were for the first time made by machines featuring monuments on the obverse. Which monument was shown on these coins?

A. The Charminar.

Q. These coins mainly the rupee, half rupee, quarter rupee, two annas were issued in 1911 with the King shown wearing a robe with a small elephant on it. These coins offended the religious sentiments of many and so were held back from circulation and later had to be melted. They had to be redesigned and circulated in 1912. What was the reason?

A. It was known as the 'Pig' rupee (the elephant did not look like one, instead it resembled a pig).

Q. As per valuation this country's reserves is equivalent to about 75 per cent of the world's gold reserves. Which is this country that has the world's highest gold reserves?

A. USA.

Q. Money changers need to be paid for changing money of one currency into another currency or for changing bank notes into cash. What is the term used for denoting this payment?

A. Agio.

Q. In 1980 Israel abolished lira as its currency and replaced it by another currency. What is the name of that currency?

A. Shekel.

Q. Agora is a denomination of Shekel and 100 agoras make 1 Shekel. What is the plural of agora?

A. Agorot.

Q. It is the means by which a government expands the economy by making money more easily available. It is done through lowering interest rates and easy access to credit. What is this government policy called?

A. Easy money policy.

Q. In Finland the markka occupied pride of place among its people till it was replaced in 1999. What is this markka?

A. The currency of Finland before euro.

Q. Elastic money is a term used in the US Federal Reserve Act. What is the meaning of this term?

A. The Act defines elastic currency as currency that can, by the actions of the central monetary authority, expand or contract in amounts as warranted by economic conditions.

Q. The guilder was the currency of the Netherlands before the euro was adopted. The Dutch guilder is known by another name as well. What is that name?

A. Florin.

Q. What is the designation of the head of the Bank of England, who is nominated by the British government?

A. Governor of Bank of England.

Q. If Governor is the designation of the Bank of England, what is the designation for the similar post of the head in the US?

A. Chairman, Federal Reserve Board

Q. Denmark has not adopted the euro as its currency even though it is part of the European Union. What is the name of its currency?

A. Danish krone.

Q. The currency of Denmark is the currency of another neighbouring European country. Which is this country?

A. Norway.

Q. It is an alphanumeric number developed for efficiency of cross-country payments. The number contains details relating to the country, bank and branch with the account number of the beneficiary. What is this number known as?

A. International Bank Account Number.

Q. IBAN is still to be adopted by all countries across the world. Which authority is responsible for creating this number?

A. European Committee for Banking Standards.

Q. Coins carry designs which are pressed into its surface. What is this design called?

A. Incuse.

Q. This educational society was formed in 1961 for promoting the study and collection of bank notes. It is a nonprofit international organization. What is the name of this organization?

A. International Bank Note Society.

Q. If a tourist is planning to visit Thailand, which currency should the visitor be carrying with him?

A. Baht.

Q. Taiwan uses the Taiwanese dollar as its currency. It is officially known as 'Xin Taibi'. What does this word mean?

A. New Taiwanese dollar.

Q. 'Renminbi' is the currency of China. What is the meaning of this word renminbi?

A. People's money.

Q. In 1945 after World War II a global currency was suggested to replace the pound sterling. It was to be managed by a global central bank. What was the name proposed for this new currency?

A. BANCOR.

Q. Money destruction meaning the reverse of money creation can occur in two different ways depending on how the money was created. The destruction of physically created money occurs when coins are scrapped. What benefit is derived from this procedure?

A. It is to recover the precious metal content of the coins.

Q. The currency of Slovenia is not the euro even though it is part of the European Union. What is the currency of Slovenia called?

A. Tolar.

Q. It is a public limited company set-up in 1995 for augmenting the production of bank notes and to bridge the gap between supply and demand for bank notes. It is located at Bengaluru with two presses at Mysore and Salboni. Name this organization?

A. Bharatiya Reserve Bank Note Mudran P. Ltd.

Q. In this ATM the hardware as well as lease is under ownership of the service provider while connectivity and cash handling and management is the responsibility of the sponsor bank. The vendor gets a fee for every transaction from the bank whose ATM card is being used. What is this type of ATM known as?

A. Brown label ATM.

Q. Indians having foreign currency (non-resident) accounts are required to have their accounts in which currency as per extant rules?

A. Any foreign currency which is fully convertible.

Q. The Indian Coinage Act had to be amended to adopt the metric system for coinage. When did the amended Act come into force?

A. 1st April, 1957.

Q. The widely used dollar symbol $ does not appear on the US currency. Which is the only symbol which is printed on the country's currency notes?

A. Pound sterling.

Q. Australia switched to the Australian dollar in 1966 as its currency. Which was the currency in use prior to this date?

A. Australian pound.

Q. What currency was Pakistan using immediately after independence in 1947 till it arranged for sufficient circulation of Pakistan currency?

A. They used Indian currency with Pakistan stamped on it.

Q. Which financial giant has a logo which resembles a Vein diagram?

A. Master Card

Q. What is the term used for a number which is the same whichever way it is read for e.g., 1441 or 2332?

A. Palindrome number.

Q. 419 scams frequently called Nigerian scams is a summary name for a large number of confidence frauds in which the victim is defrauded for monetary gain. Why are these scams given this number 419?

A. The number 419 refers to the section of the Nigerian criminal code dealing with frauds.

Q. Reserve Bank of India has minted coins under the Nritya Mudra series to serve as visual codes in quick and clear identification of rupee coins. Hand gestures from which dance form has been incorporated?

A. Bharatanatyam.

Q. Swiss banks are selling a new safe haven idea to their rich clients as per news reports. The use of this facility is reportedly outside the purview of tax treaties signed with countries which can check the clients' deposit and investment accounts. Which is this idea being proposed?

A. High value Swiss franc notes in the denomination of 1,000 to be stored in safe deposit boxes.

Q. The US economy has the maximum denomination of 100 dollars currency in circulation. It used to have high value notes like 500, 1,000 and 5,000 dollars earlier but discontinued their printing. When was it discontinued?

A. 1945 and are no longer in circulation since 1969.

Q. It is inserted into the security printing paper at the time of production which is visible on the surface of the paper at frequent intervals. It represents a reliable security element which is easily recognizable, offers high protection against counterfeiting. It is one of the major safeguards in protecting currency notes. Which security feature are we referring to?

A. Security thread.

Q. It is the Malaysian currency which is also known as the Malaysian dollar. What is the name of the currency?

A. Ringgit.

Q. The Indian rupee derives its name from the Sanskrit word 'Rupyakani' which dates the use of silver rupee coins to the sixth century BC. What is the link between the word 'rupyakani' and the currency notes?

A. The Indian currency note of today carries the Sanskrit name Rupyakani among other languages on its language panel.

Q. The rupee was once a legal tender across different countries across East Africa and Asia. Which were the countries where the rupee was accepted till 1966?

A. In Oman, Qatar and within UAE.

Q. The euro zone was formed in 1999 but the currency and coins were introduced at a later date. In which year was the euro currency and coins introduced?

A. They were introduced in 2002.

Q. The euro zone has been flexible in permitting three small states to use the euro as their official currency without being part of the euro zone. These states are not represented on the board of the European Central Bank. Can you identify these three states?

A. Monaco, San Marino and Vatican City.

Q. To become a member of the euro zone the meml ›r state has to be fulfil a certain criteria. What is the requirement?

A. To become a member the country has to spend two y‹ars in the European Exchange Rate mechanism.

Q. In an exchange rate quotation for currencies what term is used to identify the currency whose value is quoted against the base currency of value one?

A. Quoted currency.

Q. Countries which joined the euro zone had to forego their currency in favour of the euro. What was the currency of Spain prior to the euro?

A. Peseta.

Q. Punt was also the former currency of a country before being replaced by the euro. Which is that country?

A. Ireland.

Q. This is not the name of a metal but it denotes a coin in the USA of the value of 1/ 20th of a dollar. Which is this coin?

A. Nickel.

Q. A term of reference in the US Federal Reserve Act which suggests that the central monetary authority not only has the ability to expand the money supply but can also contract the money supply according to exigencies of the external environment. Which term are we referring to?

A. Elastic currency.

Q. Austral is certainly not the unit of currency in use in Australia. Which is the country which can claim it as its own?

A. Argentina.

Q. The exchange value of this currency is expected to remain stable due to robust performance of its economy. What name would you give to this currency?

A. Hard currency.

Q. ISO 4217 is the international three letter code for currencies. It is also used for other entities used in international finance. Which are these entities?

A. Precious metals like gold, silver and SDRs.

Q. Which organization is responsible for maintaining the list of codes relating to ISO 4217?

A. British Standards Institution.

Q. In most cases, each country has monopoly control over the supply and production of its own currency. Which countries are notable exceptions to this rule?

A. Member countries of the European union.

Q. Each currency has one fractional currency, often valued at 1/100th of the main currency. There are a few currencies which do not have any smaller units. Which are the countries which do not use the decimal system?

A. Mauritania and Madagascar.

■■■

QUIZ EIGHT

Finance, Accounts and Practices

Q. Which of the following would most appropriately explain the concept of Net Working Capital?

(*i*) Current assets minus current liabilities

(*ii*) Fixed assets minus current assets

(*iii*) Current assets less cash assets

(*iv*) Long-term loans less short-term loans.

A. (*i*)

Q. In the book-building process, the pricing of IPOs is based on which of the following?

(*i*) Feedback from the company

(*ii*) The response from the lead managers

(*iii*) Response from the investors

(*iv*) SEBI guidelines.

A. (*iii*)

Q. The market price of a share of common stock is finalized by which of the following ways?

(*i*) by the stock exchange on which the stock is traded

(*ii*) by the board of directors of the company

(*iii*) by the investors trading in the stock exchange

(*iv*) by the chairman of the company.

A. (*iii*)

Q. When companies and their officials debate the merits of LIFO versus FIFO what are they referring to?

(*i*) ways to recognize revenues

(*ii*) the marketing strategies to increase income

(*iii*) the comparative strengths of two comparable customer grievance handling strategies

(*iv*) the models of inventory management.

A. (*iv*)

Q. At times companies retain the net income for future use by the company and do not distribute the amount among its shareholders. What is the amount known as?

(*i*) retained earnings

(*ii*) additional assets

(*iii*) common stock

(*iv*) reserve assets.

A. (*i*)

Q. In the process of declaration and payment of dividends by a company which of the following actions occurs last in time, if arranged in chronological order?

(*i*) exdividend date

(*ii*) record date

(*iii*) dividend declaration date

(*iv*) payment date.

A. (*iv*)

Q. The shareholders' wealth in a firm is represented by which under noted expression?

(*i*) book value of the firm's assets less the book value of its liabilities

(*ii*) market price per share of the company's common stock

(*iii*) amount of salary and wages paid to the employees of the company

(*iv*) the total number of employees in the company.

A. (*i*)

Q. What does a stockholder lose when the company does not have enough assets to meet the claims of its creditors?

(*i*) the stocks face value

(*ii*) the original investment amount

(*iii*) the share of indebtedness

(*iv*) does not lose anything.

A. (*ii*)

Q. Among the following class of items which most appropriately qualifies to be the current asset of a company?

(*i*) work-in-process

(*ii*) plant and machinery

(*iii*) tax payable

(*iv*) trade debtors.

A. (*i*)

Q. Which of the following would not qualify as a debt instrument as referred in financial transactions?

(*i*) certificates of deposit

(*ii*) bonds

(*iii*) stocks

(*iv*) commercial papers.

A. (*iii*)

Q. Which of the following is not considered to be a part of the annual reports and accounts of a limited company?

(*i*) cash flow statement

(*ii*) profit and loss account

(*iii*) balance sheet

(*iv*) projected cash flow.

A. (*iv*)

Q. Except one all others are financial markets. Which is the exception of the following?

(*i*) pension fund market

(*ii*) foreign exchange market

(*iii*) money market

(*iv*) fixed income market.

A. (*i*)

Q. In the case of a professional corporation, which of the following has limited liability?

(*i*) only the professionals

(*ii*) only the business

(*iii*) both the professionals and the business

(*iv*) neither business nor the professionals.

A. (*ii*)

Q. Companies are known to provide shareholders returns from———, while capital markets generate returns to shareholders from ———?

(*i*) capital gains, dividends

(*ii*) appreciation, capital gains

(*iii*) dividends, capital gains

(*iv*) earnings, capital appreciation.

A. (*iii*)

Q. In a company the use of price sensitive corporate information by the staff to make unexpected gains is known as?

(*i*) insider trading

(*ii*) future trading

(*iii*) stock trading

(*iv*) foreign trading.

A. (*i*)

Q. The formal or institutional credit delivery system in the rural areas of the country is handled by the following institutions:

(*a*) cooperative credit societies

(*b*) commercial banks

(*c*) regional rural banks

(*d*) self-help groups.

Which of the following option is the correct one?

(*i*) only (*a*) and (*b*)

(*ii*) only (*c*) and (*d*)

(*iii*) only (*a*) , (*b*) and (*c*)

(*iv*) all of the above.

A. (*iv*)

Q. What is the term used for the budgeting exercise which is based on what happened the previous year?

(*i*) zero budgeting

(*ii*) historical budgeting

(*iii*) flexible budgeting

(*iv*) careless budgeting.

A. (*ii*)

Q. Companies often sell new shares to the existing shareholders in proportion to their shareholding in the company. What is this practice known as?

(*i*) new issue

(*ii*) rights issue

(*iii*) preference issue

(*iv*) floating issue.

A. (*ii*)

Q. At times a dividend is paid to shareholders in the form of new shares instead of cash payments. What is this dividend called?

(*i*) equity dividend

(*ii*) scrip dividend

(*iii*) rights dividend

(*iv*) deferred dividend.

A. (*ii*)

Q. Gross profit would be explained most effectively by which of the following statements?

(*i*) sales less cost of sales

(*ii*) sales less operating costs

(*iii*) sales less depreciation

(*iv*) cash receipts less expenses.

A. (*i*)

Q. How would you express retained profit by choosing one of the options?

(*i*) profit after tax less dividends

(*ii*) sales less cost of sales

(*iii*) operating profit plus dividends

(*iv*) gross profits less overheads.

A. (*i*)

Q. The amount by which the total costs increase with the production of one additional unit is known as:

(*i*) fixed costs

(*ii*) variable costs

(*iii*) marginal costs

(*iv*) cost benefit.

A. (*iii*)

Q. Which of the following defines the costs that change in proportion to the amount of output produced?

(*i*) fixed costs

(*ii*) variable costs

(*iii*) overhead costs

(*iv*) depreciation.

A. (*ii*)

Q. Which of the following would you consider as the important service to investors provided by mutual funds?

(*i*) the scope to invest in corporate securities at preferential prices

(*ii*) a better rate of return

(*iii*) diversification

(*iv*) high expenses and trading costs which increase the rate of return.

A. (*iii*)

Q. Which of the following would be considered an advantage of the sole proprietorship form of constitution for an enterprise?

(*i*) wide access to capital markets

(*ii*) pool of expertise and skills

(*iii*) profits taxed at only one level

(*iv*) unlimited liability.

A. (*iii*)

Q. Owners of mutual funds own ———, and are called ————?

(*i*) deposits, depositors

(*ii*) bonds, bondholders

(*iii*) shares, shareholders

(*iv*) units of mutual funds, creditors.

A. (*iii*)

Q. Which of the following assets would not be categorized as a current asset?

(*i*) trade debtors

(*ii*) plant and machinery

(*iii*) cash in hand

(*iv*) stocks.

A. (*ii*)

Q. Which of the following performance measures would be of most direct interest to shareholders?

(*i*) gross profit margin

(*ii*) return on net assets

(*iii*) stock turnover

(*iv*) dividend yield.

A. (*iv*)

Q. The first time that a security is sold it is in——— market, subsequently trading of the security is in———market:

(*i*) money, capital

(*ii*) capital, money

(*iii*) banking, secondary

(*iv*) primary, secondary.

A. (*iv*)

Q. Of the following expenditures which would be reckoned as an example of capital expenditure?

(*i*) spending on factory equipment

(*ii*) spending on raw materials

(*iii*) spending on machine maintenance

(*iv*) spending on wages and salaries.

A. (*i*)

Q. Which of the following ratios explain the definition of market price per share divided by earnings per share?

(*i*) accounts receivable turnover

(*ii*) inventory turnover

(*iii*) price earnings ratio

(*iv*) debt equity ratio.

A. (*iii*)

Q. Which of the following is an example of long-term liability?

(*i*) bank loan due for payment in 3 years period

(*ii*) accruals for year end costs

(*iii*) dividends payable

(*iv*) bank overdraft payable.

A. (*i*)

Q. The accounting reduction in the original value of a fixed asset over the useful life is known as:

(*i*) obsolescence

(*ii*) disposal

(*iii*) devaluation

(*iv*) depreciation.

A. (*iv*)

Q. Price to earnings ratio is calculated in which of the following ways?

(*i*) dividing sales by net profit

(*ii*) dividing market price of shares by earnings per share

(*iii*) dividing market price of share by book value

(*iv*) dividing book value by earnings per share.

A. (*ii*)

Q. The money market is a ————market, while the capital market is a————market:

(*i*) investment, liquidity

(*ii*) short-term, long-term
(*iii*) liquidity, financial investment
(*iv*) long-term, short-term.

A. (*ii*)

Q. The amount that can be realized by a company if it sells its business as an active and operating enterprise would be treated as:

(*i*) market value
(*ii*) book value
(*iii*) going concern value
(*iv*) replacement value.

A. (*iii*)

Q. Financial ratios are classified under different categories while analyzing balance sheet of a business. Which of the following would be treated as a liquidity ratio?

(*i*) return on equity
(*ii*) acid test ratio
(*iii*) debt equity ratio
(*iv*) return on capital.

A. (*ii*)

Q. The interest rate which is specified on a fixed maturity security at the time of issue is known as:

(*i*) market rate of interest
(*ii*) call rate
(*iii*) coupon rate
(*iv*) repo rate.

A. (*iii*)

Q. The balance sheet of a business enterprise denotes the financial position at a given point of time. How would the balance sheet equation be defined as?

(*i*) liabilities equals assets plus equity
(*ii*) assets equals equity plus liabilities
(*iii*) assets divided by equity equals liabilities
(*iv*) assets plus liabilities equals equity.

A. (*ii*)

Q. The balance sheet of a company is prepared to serve which of the following purposes?

(*i*) measure the company's performance over a period of time
(*ii*) determine the taxes due and payable

(*iii*) indicate the company's value as of a given point of time

(*iv*) to balance the company's assets and liabilities.

A. (*iii*)

Q. The Planning Commission of India was constituted in which year?

(*i*) 1947

(*ii*) 1950

(*iii*) 1952

(*iv*) 1965

A. (*ii*)

Q. Who coined the term 'Hindu rate of Growth' for the Indian economy?

(*i*) Amartya Sen

(*ii*) Y V Reddy

(*iii*) Montek Singh

(*iv*) Raj Krishna

A. (*iv*)

Q. Which of the following is a depository in the country for handling shares in the demat form?

(*i*) NSDL

(*ii*) RBI

(*iii*) MCX

(*iv*) SEBI

A. (*i*)

Q. Which of the following is not considered as a means of foreign capital inflow into the country?

(*i*) Foreign Direct Investment

(*ii*) FCNR accounts

(*iii*) Foreign Institutional Investors

(*iv*) No frills accounts

A. (*iv*)

Q. In the exchange rate quoted for the rupee against the US dollar which is identified as the base currency?

(*i*) the rupee

(*ii*) both are base currencies

(*iii*) neither

(*iv*) the US dollar

A. (*iv*)

Q. When Indian companies raise funds overseas what is the process known as?

(*i*) participatory notes

(*ii*) foreign currency non-resident accounts

(*iii*) foreign currency convertible bonds

(*iv*) nostro accounts

A. (*iii*)

Q. Which of the following is not considered to be part of costing?

(*i*) opportunity cost

(*ii*) prime cost

(*iii*) office and administration cost

(*iv*) factory overheads

A. (*i*)

Q. Which type of ratios is a measure of the liquidity of specific assets and the efficiency of managing assets of a company?

(*i*) liquidity ratios

(*ii*) profitability ratios

(*iii*) leverage ratios

(*iv*) activity ratios

A. (*iv*)

Q. Which of the following financial ratios best defines the time taken by customers to settle bills with regard to an enterprise?

(*i*) creditors days

(*ii*) debtor days

(*iii*) stock turnover

(*iv*) acid test ratio

A. (*ii*)

Q. Shares of a company can be issued by which of the following ways?

(*i*) at par

(*ii*) at premium

(*iii*) at discount

(*iv*) all of the above

A. (*iv*)

Q. Which of the following is an item of capital expenditure?

(*i*) insurance premium paid for plant and machinery

(*ii*) VAT paid for purchase of office furniture

(*iii*) Interest on loan paid for furniture and fixtures

(*iv*) Monthly rent instalment paid for the machine taken on hire purchase system

A. (*ii*)

Q. In a balance sheet which of the following is assumed to be the least liquid asset?

(*i*) trade debtors

(*ii*) stocks/inventory

(*iii*) short-term investments

(*iv*) cash balances

A. (*ii*)

Q. Which of the following items would be considered as a category or element of the balance sheet of a company?

(*i*) expenses

(*ii*) losses

(*iii*) liabilities

(*iv*) gains

A. (*iii*)

Q. Which of the following options would constitute the two main parts of the equity half of the balance sheet?

(*i*) share capital and retained profits

(*ii*) current assets and current liabilities

(*iii*) non-current assets and current assets

(*iv*) long-term liabilities and shares

A. (*i*)

Q. Which type of financial ratios would reflect the degree to which the business is already financed by borrowed funds?

(*i*) liquidity ratios

(*ii*) leverage ratios

(*iii*) turnover ratios

(*iv*) profitability ratios

A. (*ii*)

Q. Which of the following appropriately defines the net trade cycle?

(*i*) the amount of time needed to complete the normal operating cycle of a firm

(*ii*) the amount of time it takes to manufacture or purchase inventory (*iii*) the amount of time it takes to sell inventory

(*iv*) none of the above

A. (*i*)

Q. Which of the following documents is not included in annual financial statements of a company?

(*i*) profit and loss account

(*ii*) balance sheet

(*iii*) cash flow statement

(*iv*) directors' report

A. (*iii*)

Q. Which of the following entities is not permitted to speak in the Annual General Meeting of a company?

(*i*) director

(*ii*) auditor

(*iii*) proxy

(*iv*) all of the above

A. (*ii*)

Q. Analysing debt to equity ratio of a company gives a measure of?

(*i*) financial leverage

(*ii*) operating leverage

(*iii*) profitability

(*iv*) liquidity

A. (*i*)

Q. Depreciation on fixed assets is an approved practice in accounting. Which of the following explains depreciation on fixed assets?

(*i*) source of funds

(*ii*) use of funds

(*iii*) no flow of fund

(*iv*) all of the above

A. (*iv*)

Q. Watered capital of the company is explained by which of the following?

(*i*) undercapitalization

(*ii*) overcapitalization

(*iii*) that part of capital which is not presented through assets

(*iv*) unissued capital

A. (*iii*)

Q. The current ratio for a company for three consecutive years worked out to be 1:2, 0:90 and 0:60 respectively. What do these figures indicate?

(*i*) the company is using current assets in a better way

(*ii*) the liquidity of the company is worsening

(*iii*) the bank finance has been paid-off

(*iv*) there has been a large-scale sale of current assets

A. (*ii*)

Q. Which of the following would indicate why it is important to calculate cash flows?

(*i*) firms need cash to serve debt, dividends, expenses

(*ii*) companies that generate healthy profits may be unable to convert profits into cash

(*iii*) cash flow ratios help the analyst assess the long-term profitability of a firm

(*iv*) both (*i*) and (*ii*)

A. (*iv*)

Q. What is the ratio which is defined by total liabilities divided by shareholders' equity?

(*i*) inventory turnover

(*ii*) debt equity ratio

(*iii*) accounts receivable turnover

(*iv*) price earnings ratio

A. (*ii*)

Q. Which of the following would best explain the term asset turnover?

(*i*) ratio of credit sales to total assets

(*ii*) ratio of sales to total assets

(*iii*) ratio of cost of goods sold to total assets

(*iv*) none of the above

A. (*ii*)

Q. How would you explain the term interest coverage ratio?

(*i*) ratio of operating income to interest expenses

(*ii*) ratio of interest income to interest expenses

(*iii*) ratio of gross profit to operating profit

(*iv*) ratio of net income to interest income

A. (*i*)

Q. What does a decreasing inventory turnover ratio usually indicate about a company?

(*i*) the company is selling more inventory

(*ii*) the company is managing its inventory well

(*iii*) the firm is inefficient in the management of inventory

(*iv*) both (*i*) and (*ii*)

A. (*iii*)

Q. The stock turnover ratio is calculated using which of the following formulae?

(*i*) stock to annual sales

(*ii*) gross profit margin to operating profit margin

(*iii*) cost of goods sold to average stocks held

(*iv*) average revenues to year end stocks

A. (*iii*)

Q. In which of the following instances is the working capital being managed best?

(*i*) creditors days ratio is higher than stock turnover ratio

(*ii*) creditors days ratio is higher than debtors days ratio

(*iii*) stock turnover and creditors days ratio are both similar

(*iv*) creditors days ratio is lower than debtors days ratio

A. (*ii*)

Q. Return on capital employed would be best expressed by which of the following as a percentage?

(*i*) profit before interest and tax divided by capital x 100

(*ii*) profit after tax and dividend divided by capital x 100

(*iii*) gross profit divided by capital employed x 100

(*iv*) sales divided by capital employed x 100

A. (*i*)

Q. Which of the following appropriately defines net worth?

(*i*) the value of your home less the amount due on the home loan

(*ii*) the money left every month from salary after payment of domestic expenses

(*iii*) the money you have after deducting your dues

(*iv*) the total value of your assets minus your liabilities

A. (*iv*)

Q. Which of the following is not considered while calculating the credit score of a borrower?

(*i*) type of credit

(*ii*) outstanding debt

(*iii*) payment history

(*iv*) income

A. (*iv*)

Q. Which option explains the purchase of shares and bonds of Indian companies by foreign institutional investors?

(*i*) foreign direct investment

(*ii*) non-resident investment

(*iii*) portfolio investment

(*iv*) foreign indirect investment

A. (*i*)

Q. The Government of India is empowered to borrow any amount of funds it likes from RBI through which of the following instruments?

(*i*) commercial papers

(*ii*) treasury bills

(*iii*) certificates of deposits

(*iv*) none of the above

A. (*ii*)

Q. In India which of the following are a part of legal tender money?

(*i*) coins and currency notes

(*ii*) coins and bank drafts

(*iii*) only currency issued by RBI

(*iv*) currency and SDR

A. (*i*)

Q. What is that agreement under which an issuing bank at the request of the buyer/importer undertakes to make payment to the seller/exporter against specified documents?

(*i*) bill of exchange

(*ii*) letter of credit

(*iii*) bill of lading

(*iv*) letter of exchange

A. (*ii*)

Q. Fiat money is defined as the money which is:

(*i*) accepted in all international transactions

(*ii*) accepted as a security in lieu of gold

(*iii*) decreed as money by the government

(*iv*) issued by keeping gold as security

A. (*iii*)

Q. It is the presentation of an account showing the finances of a company written out in the form of two lines in the shape of a T. The title of the account is indicated above the top horizontal line and the debits appear on the left side of the other vertical line with credits on the right. What is the name given to such presentation?

A. T-Account.

Q. It is the rate at which the German central bank Bundesbank lends funds to the commercial banks. Name it?

A. Lombard rate.

Q. We are referring to legislation passed in the USA in 2002 to check aggressive accounting practices which led to a series of scandals. It was meant to increase transparency in accounting practices by creating the Public Accounting Oversight Board to regulate the working of accounting firms providing audit services. Which was this legislation?

A. Sarbanes Oxley Act, 2002.

Q. It is an accounting trick to make the leverage ratios of companies look better. Lehman Bros. the finance company in the USA used this gimmick to fudge their accounts during the crisis of 2008 leading to their collapse. This accounting jugglery is used by companies to classify a short-term loan as sales proceeds and later use the funds from this said sale to reduce its liabilities. Which is this accounting practice that gives a completely distorted picture of the balance sheet of the company?

A. Repo 105.

■■■

QUIZ NINE

Personalities and Happenings

Q. The most influential business people like chief executives and heads of finance of the top 10,000 most successful companies in the world are identified by a special name. What is the term used for this exclusive club?

A. C suite.

Q. Identify the hedge fund founder of the Galleon group who was convicted for insider trading in the US?

A. Raj Rajaratnam.

Q. The sculptures of Yaksha and Yakshini flank the entrance of the New Delhi office of the Reserve Bank of India. Yaksha and Yakshini are linked to which Hindu God?

A. Lord Kubera.

Q. Nick Leeson became a household name when his financial deals lead to the crash of the oldest bank in England. Which was this bank?

A. Barings Bank.

Q. The Narasimhan committee report of the 1990s changed the face of Indian banking. What background did the Chairman of this committee have?

A. He was an ex-Governor of the Reserve Bank of India.

Q. Shroffs, sahukars, chettiars are often mentioned in the context of the evolution of banking in India. What role did they perform?

A. They were known as indigenous bankers who performed a critical role of providing credit to the large population in India when banking was still to grow.

Q. He is popular as 'Voldemart' and 'London Whale' because of his clout in London banking circles and the size of his trading positions. He reportedly caused a 2 billion US dollar trading loss to his company. Can you identify the individual?

A. Bruno Michel Iksil, the French trader who caused the loss to J P Morgan.

Q. Three traders of French origin have been linked to losses running into billions of dollars for these banks. Besides Iksil, the other two are Jerome Kerviel and Fabrice Tourre. Which were the institutions that were affected?

A. Kerviel cost Societe Generale nearly 7 billion US dollars in 2006-07 and Tourre caused Goldman Sachs half a billion US dollars loss.

Q. In 1991 the foreign exchange reserves of India had reached its lowest point. The amount of reserves was just sufficient to meet the cost of three weeks worth of imports. What was the actual balance of foreign exchange reserves?

A. 3.96 billion US dollars of reserves.

Q. The terms 'macroeconomics' and 'microeconomics' were coined by which individual?

A. Ragner Frisch.

Q. Which policy decision of the Indian government permitted the public sector banks to access the capital markets?

A. Narasimhan Committee Report 1991.

Q. The Tequila crisis of 1994-95 was a result of the sudden devaluation of the currency of a country in one of the emerging market economies. Which was this country?

A. Mexico.

Q. Who has been the longest serving Reserve Bank of India Governor?

A. Sir Benegal Rama Rau was at the helm of RBI from 1st July, 1949 to 14th January, 1957.

Q. The term BRIC was coined sometime in 2001 to denote the economies of Brazil, Russia, India and China as the fastest growing among the emerging market economies. Who is credited with coining this word?

A. Jim O'Neill of Goldman Sachs.

Q. With the slow down of the economies of the BRIC nations another set of countries have been identified recently which are showing significant signs of progress. These countries are identified by the term MIST. Which are these countries?

A. MIST refers to Mexico, Indonesia, South Korea and Turkey.

Q. It is considered as the largest counterfeiting operation in history and has been fictionalized in books, films. It was a secret Nazi plan devised during the Second World War to destabilize the British economy by flooding the country with forged Bank of England currency notes of 5, 10, 20 and 50 pound sterling denomination. What was the code name of this operation?

A. Operation Bernhard.

Q. Who said "If you owe the bank $ 100 that's your problem. If you owe the bank $ 100 million, that's the bank's problem".

A. J P Getty.

Q. Who is considered as the first billionaire in the USA?

A. John D Rockefeller who founded the Standard Oil Company in 1870.

Q. Who said 'No generation has a right to contract debts greater than that can be paid-off during the course of its own existence'.

A. US President Thomas Jefferson in 1789.

Q. The Bank of England on Threadneedle Street in London has the statue of a prominent member of the Royal family. Whose statue are we talking about?

A. Duke of Wellington.

Q. Occupy Wall Street movement was a campaign against rising economic inequality in the society. It stirred the population across the Western countries and became a huge social movement. Which publication is responsible for proposing this idea?

A. Adbusters from Canada.

Q. It was started in the Netherlands in 1436 and was termed as a painless form of taxation. Queen Elizabeth also used it to raise money for public good. Can you connect the available information to identify what we are talking about?

A. The game of lottery.

Q. Who is famously known as the Big Bull of Indian stock markets and was responsible for the stock market scam of the 1990s?

A. Harshad Mehta.

Q. He is known as an economist who is backing his prediction for a global 'perfect storm' in 2013. He is often dubbed as 'Dr Doom' for predicting the 2008 crisis, the debt crisis in Europe and other adverse economic events in the world. Can you identify him?

A. Nouriel Roubini.

Q. Who is regarded as the first President of the World Bank?

A. Eugene Mayer in 1946.

Q. He was the Chief of the International Monetary Fund and was a likely contender for the post of President of France. His career came to an abrupt end because of his involvement in a sex scandal. Who is this personality?

A. Dominique Strauss Kahn.

Q. 'Every man of ambition has to fight this century with its own weapons. What this century worships is wealth. The God of this century is wealth. To succeed one must have wealth. At all costs one must have wealth.' This was said by a very well known literary person in the 19th century. Who is this personality?

A. Oscar Wilde.

Q. Reserve Bank of India was established on 1st April, 1935. Who was the first Governor to head the Reserve Bank of India?

A. Sir Osborne Smith.

Q. Talking of junk bonds and the stock market crash of the 1980s which individual comes to mind. He was also indicted for insider trading. Which is this individual?

A. Michael Milken.

Q. In Hindu mythology Lakshmi is known as the Goddess of Fortune. Who is regarded as the God of Wealth?

A. Kubera.

Q. One of the world's largest treasure troves was discovered in the late 19th century on the banks of the river Oxus in the Republic of Tajikistan in Soviet Central Asia. This hoard is currently in the British Museum, London. This treasure has a very well known name. What is it?

A. 'Oxus Treasure'.

Q. The root of this word is 'weal' which means well-being, sound, healthy. Which is this word which is the cornerstone of finance?

A. Wealth.

Q. While discussing financial inclusion and the spread of banking, there is invariably a reference to M Pesa which is considered as a success story in Kenya. What does M Pesa relate to?

A. It is the mobile based remittance facility in use in Kenya.

Q. The Wall Street journal belongs to this group along side the ownership of well known stock market indices in the US. Which is this group?

A. Dow and Jones.

Q. Which financial services group carries the tag as 'the Thundering Herd'?

A. Merrill Lynch.

Q. Commemorative stamps on famous personalities are issued to highlight their achievements. One such personality was the first foreigner to appear on British stamps. Who is this Indian individual?

A. Mohandas Karamchand Gandhi.

Q. Which bank in India opened a special account designated as '2611' for people to deposit fund for the 26/11 victims of Mumbai?

A. AXIS Bank.

Q. The account of a former President of India has been kept active in a Patna branch of the Punjab National Bank. It was opened on 24th October, 1962. Identify the former President in whose name this accounts exists?

A. Dr. Rajendra Prasad, the first President of independent India.

Q. Rajat Gupta has been indicted for insider trading by an US court. Which prosecutor of Indian origin proved the charges against him?

A. Preet Bharara.

Q. This German family of a father and five sons started their financial business in the 18th century and grew into a finance house of enormous influence and clout. They were synonymous with endless wealth and extravagant lifestyles. They financed wars and are reported to have the largest net worth in modern history. Identify this family?

A. The Rothschild family.

Q. He is one of the most successful financial speculators of our time. Some one who is most envied and feared in the world of hedge funds. He set-up SAC Capital. His wife reportedly gifted him an ATM on his birthday because he kept borrowing money from her. Connect the facts to identify the man?

A. Steven A Cohen.

Q. Who said 'My wealth comes from luck and compound interest'.

A. Warren Buffet.

Q. Goldman Sachs the internationally famous investment bank was founded in New York in 1869 by Goldman. He was later joined by his son-in-law in 1882. Can you name both the gentlemen?

A. Marcus Goldman and Samuel Sachs.

Q. 'The buck stops with the guy who signs the cheque' … Who is reported to have made this statement?

A. Rupert Murdoch the well known news baron.

Q. A very well known Indian entrepreneur who started his business in 1981 is the son of a school teacher. He is reported to have been detained by the police in Belgium for talking about capitalism. Who is this individual?

A. Narayana Murthy.

Q. Mark Zuckerberg recently came out with the public issue of Facebook. It fared poorly at the stock markets. How did he react the day after the IPO botched?

A. Mark married his girlfriend.

Q. He is the author of the largest selling book *'Economics: An Introductory Analysis'* and also the first American to win the Nobel prize in Economics. Who are we talking about?

A. Paul Samuelson.

Q. In which year was the Railway budget first presented in British India?

A. 1924.

Q. Warren Buffet is known to have distributed newspapers while he was in his teens. Which newspaper did he deliver and later held as an investment?

A. *Washington Post.*

Q. "It's the economy, stupid" is the famous line of a political campaign manager during the election of the US President. This line has since become the most important defining issue in every US election. During the election of which US President was this statement made?

A. Bill Clinton.

Q. He is reported to have made over 1 billion US dollars by betting on the devaluation of the pound sterling in 1992. He is referred to as 'the man who broke the Bank of England'. Identify the person being referred to?

A. George Soros.

Q. In 1850 Mayer joined the business run by his siblings Henry and Emanuel. The company did exceedingly well in the world of finance till it collapsed. Which company are we talking about?

A. Lehman Brothers.

Q. Davos in Switzerland was the venue of the annual meeting of the World Economic Forum for 31 years. However in 2002 it moved to a new venue. Where and why did they move?

A. New York was the venue as a gesture of solidarity in the wake of 9/11 attacks.

Q. He is the former Governor of the Reserve Bank of India and also the author of the book *'Global Crisis, Recession and Uneven Recovery'*. Can you name him?

A. Y V Reddy.

Q. Hurricane Sandy created havoc in New York recently. It became the cause for the closure of this important institution after the previous one Gloria. Which is this institution under reference?

A. New York Stock Exchange.

Q. It is a well known Hindu festival celebrated for bringing good fortune. It derives its name from the mix of the words 'wealth' and a numerical figure. Which is this festival?

A. Dhanteras.

Q. Hire purchase is a popular mode of financing consumer durables. Which company is credited to have originated this particular financing technique to push its sales?

A. Singer company.

Q. Marcus Aguis the former Chairman of Barclays Bank had to resign from his post in the wake of the financial scandal that the Bank faced. What was this issue?

A. The complicity of Barclays Bank in the reported manipulation of the LIBOR over an extended period of time.

Q. He was India's first finance minister from 1947 to 1949 and presented the first Union Budget. Who is this individual?

A. R Shanmukham Chetty.

Q. 'Gold is money, everything else is credit'...this was the statement of which well known person to the US Congress in 1912?

A. J P Morgan.

Q. In order to become a full-time financial services business, this company decided to drop its 155 years old telegram service. Which company are we talking about?

A. Western Union.

Q. In the context of free services it is often stated that there are no free lunches or nothing comes free. Which economist has written a book with the title *"There's no such thing as a free lunch"*?

A. Milton Friedman.

Q. Can you identify the well known financial services provider which is popular for its tag line 'Never leave home without it'?

A. *American Express* for its credit cards.

Q. The famous online lottery business 'Sixo' in Kerala was run by a controversial personality known for his interest in sports. Name this individual?

A. Lalit Modi.

Q. The term 'animal spirits' is often mentioned by politicians and economists to revive sagging spirits and slow moving economies. Who is credited with coining this term?

A. John Maynard Keynes, the economist.

Q. They are so famous that they are referred to in finance textbooks simply as 'MM'. They are known to have given the solution to the issue of the restricted case of perfect markets. Who are these persons?

A. Franco Modigliani and Merton Miller.

Q. Which financial institution launched the world's first index fund in 1973 which were meant primarily for institutional investors?

A. Wells Fargo of the US established the Standard & Poor's composite index fund.

Q. Ten bagger is a term used to indicate a stock whose value increases ten times its purchase price. This expression was used by a famous investor in his book *'One up on Wall Street'*. Which is this personality?

A. Peter Lynch.

Q. A new form of micro lending that is based on the peer-to-peer lending model has proved extremely successful online. They are known for their 25 dollar loan. Which is this world's largest P2P lending platform based in the US?

A. Kiva of San Francisco, USA.

Q. In India an online platform is available which enables people to choose borrowers from a list of micro loan seekers from across the country. This is the new form of electronic micro lending. Who has popularized this concept?

A. Rangde.

Q. This politician has an Indian army background. He joined politics and became India's finance minister at one time. Who is he?

A. Jaswant Singh.

Q. The Glass Steagall Act in the US is instrumental in segregating investment banking from commercial banking to prevent unethical investment practices and financial crisis. When and why was this law enacted?

A. It was after the Great Depression of 1929-33 that this law was considered necessary.

Q. Which well known insurance company in the US had to be nationalized during the 2008 economic crisis?

A. American International Group (AIG)

Q. A well known English bank suffered a bank run in 2007 when its customers queued outside its branches to withdraw cash prompting it to seek support from the Bank of England. Which bank in England faced this situation?

A. Northern Rock.

Q. In 1860 which British official became the first Auditor General of India?

A. Sir Edward Drummond.

Q. Dow Jones Industrial Average is the well known stock market index of the US. Which company's stock is the oldest component of DJIA index. It is present in this index since 1907?

A. General Electric Company.

Q. Banking in India has evolved and made significant progress as a result of the contribution of certain industrialists and business families of the southern part of India. Infact, a certain geographical area in South India is named as the 'cradle of Indian banking'. Which is this area?

A. Undivided Kannada district.

Q. This location is in a valley in the US state of Wyoming which has been the venue of the Federal Reserve's annual symposium every year since 1978. Can you name this place?

A. Jackson Hole.

Q. In 1995 an international organization was created to facilitate free trade among nations by removing restrictive trade practices. Which is this organization?

A. World Trade Organization (WTO).

Q. Scott Sullivan was released in 2009 after a five year jail term in USA. He was accused of fraudulent activities due to which investors lost billions of dollars. What was his offence?

A. He managed one of the largest accounting frauds in US history.

Q. Which two famous personalities are considered to be the founding fathers of the International Monetary Fund?

A. John Maynard Keynes and Harry Dexter.

Q. The Ponzi scheme of Bernie Madoff dumped large number of people. Which famous celebrity from the Hollywood allegedly lost US $ 10 million?

A. Zsa Zsa Gabor.

Q. Henry Brown was an investor who saw a convenient and secure way to store money, valuables and important papers. He developed a suitable storing mechanism which he patented in 1886. What did he invent?

A. The strong box.

Q. The vacancy for this post was advertised globally and he happens to be the first non-British to be appointed. Who is the person who has been selected for this important financial position in England?

A. Mark Carney has been appointed as the Governor of Bank of England.

Q. Jamie Dimon continues to head this bank even though it made US $ 2 billion trading losses currently. Which is this bank which largely remained unaffected during the sub-prime crisis of 2008?

A. JP Morgan Chase Bank.

Q. This bank has paid a fine of about US $ 450 million to the US and UK regulators for its involvement in the LIBOR scandal. Its chief executive also quit office amid the discontent owing to the scandal. Which is this bank?

A. Barclays Bank.

Q. Where in the world would you find the highest ATM centre?

A. Sikkim.

Q. The daily cheque clearing began around 1770 when bank clerks met at a tavern to exchange all their cheques in one place and settle the balance in cash. Which is that place where it first started?

A. At the Five Bells a tavern in London.

Q. The banking ombudsman has become an important authority in the grievance redressal machinery for bank services. This concept of the ombudsman was first initiated in which country?

A. Sweden.

Q. A German bank Sparkasse Chemitz is issuing a Master Card with a very unusual image for a credit card. Whose image is it?

A. Karl Marx.

Q. Ben Mezrich's book *The Accidental Billionaires* is about Facebook. Which recent movie is based on Facebook?

A. The Social Network.

Q. The US is facing a financial impasse owing to the debt ceiling for the government which needs to be raised. Which is the only other country which has a debt ceiling?

A. Denmark.

Q. Reserve Bank of India has organized programmes to increase awareness about technology enabled financial services. What is the name given to these programmes?

A. e BAAT electronic Banking Awareness and Training.

Q. This industrialist recently donated 3 kg of gold to Lord Venkateshwara of Tirupati probably seeking divine help for his company in deep financial crisis. Which is this industrialist?

A. Vijay Mallya of Kingfisher Airlines.

Q. Mukesh Ambani is reported to have spent over US $ 1 billion towards constructing his 27 storey residential building in Mumbai. What is the name of this building?

A. Antilla.

Q. It started in 1882 as a niche news agency to become a world class publication of business news and information. They are the owners of Wall Street journal and stock index. Which agency are we talking about?

A. Dow Jones.

Q. This market index helps investors weigh social and environmental factors in making choices. It is an index comprising of chiefly large capitalized stocks of 400 publicly listed companies in the S&P 500. Which is this index?

A. Domino Social 400 index.

Q. He is a Nobel prize winning economist who devised the modern portfolio theory in 1952. His work changed the way people invested. Who is this economist?

A. Harry Markowitz.

Q. Known as Fannie Mae it is a US government sponsored enterprise that was created in 1938 to expand the flow of mortgage money by creating a secondary mortgage market. How is this body officially known as?

A. Federal National Mortgage Association.

Q. He remained Chairman of the Board of Governors of the Federal Reserve for an unusually lengthy period of eighteen years. He is also known to have controlled the stock market crisis of the US in 1987 and the dot com bubble in the early 2000s. Who is this personality?

A. Alan Greenspan.

Q. Nations when they reach self-sufficiency tend to dissociate from external trade and commerce thereby isolating itself. This is not a welcome step in view of greater interaction among countries. What is this state of a nation known as?

A. Autarky.

Q. He is known to be an Indian Scottish who is regarded to be the inventor of the automated teller machine. Can you name him?

A. Adrian Shepherd Barron.

Q. It started as a commercial bank and was later nationalized in 1946. It became independent in 1997 and remains the central bank of the country. Which is this institution?

A. Bank of England.

Q. He is the regarded as the finance minister of the country. He is equivalent to the Treasury Secretary in the US. What is the name of this post in England?

A. Chancellor of the Exchequer.

Q. In the words of the writer the Darwinian law of the survival of the fittest applies to financial institutions as well. Only those institutions which have a selfish gene to replicate itself and self-perpetuate, can only endure. Which writer are we talking about?

A. Niall Ferguson in 'Ascent of Money'.

Q. Frank McNamara faced embarrassment when he was dining with his friends. It was in 1950 that he decided to have a brand which would address such awkward moments. Which brand are we talking about?

A. Diners Club.

Q. He is considered the 'Godfather' of mortgage finance for his role in pioneering securitization and mortgage based securities. Though he was regarded as one of the greatest innovators of the last 75 years, he is also held responsible for the financial crisis in 2007. Whom are we talking about?

A. Lewis S Ranieri.

Q. An American business executive who was Chairman and CEO of Goldman Sachs Group rose to become the Secretary of the US Treasury from 2006-09. He pushed the Federal Reserve takeover of the government mortgage loan agencies and also created a credit facility that enabled the insurance corporation American International Group to avoid bankruptcy. Who is this well known personality?

A. Henry Paulson.

Q. 'The highest use of capital is not to make more money, but to make money do more for the betterment of life.' He was a famous American capitalist and pioneer of mass production. He had a commitment towards philanthropy. Name this individual who said these words.

A. Henry Ford.

Q. The following quotation is of a former US President delivered at a University gathering in December 2000:

'No generation has had the opportunity as we now have, to build a global economy that leaves no one behind. It is a wonderful opportunity, but also a profound responsibility.' Can you identify him?

A. Bill Clinton.

Q. He is known as an outstanding poet and thinker of yesteryears. He is quoted to say: 'Money is like love; it kills slowly and painfully the one who holds it'. Name the poet?

A. Khalil Gibran.

Q. When was the Nobel Prize for Economics first given and to whom?

A. In 1969 to Ragner Frisch and Jan Tinbergen.

Q. The Liikanen Report on European Union banking reforms has been submitted in October 2012. It relates to the recommendations as to whether the structural reforms of European Union Banks would strengthen financial stability and improve efficiency. Can you identify Liikanen who was responsible for the report?

A. Erkki Liikanen is the Governor of Finland's central bank.

Q. The Basel-I recommendations were adopted in1988. Federal Reserve Governor Daniel Tarullo wrote in his 2008 book *'Banking on Basel'* that Basel-I came about because the US and Europe were alarmed by the expansion of Japan's financial clout. What Japanese strength were they disturbed about?

A. At that time 9 out of 10 largest banks in the world were Japanese.

Q. Recently 32 tax evaders in UK have been sentenced to a combined total of 155 years and 10 months behind bars. The UK tax agency has adopted a new move to shame tax dodgers as part of their crack down on tax evasion. What is the strategy they have adopted?

A. They have published the names and photographs of 2012's top tax cheats.

Q. Named after a Nobel Prize winning economist, the idea was first proposed in 1978 of a tax on foreign exchange transactions that would be applied uniformly by all major countries. It would be a charge levied on all foreign currency exchange transactions to deter speculation on currency. The tax carried the name of which economist?

A. Tobin Tax named after James Tobin.

Q. Satoshi Nakamoto, a computer programmer introduced a digital currency in 2009 which is bought and sold electronically through a peer-to-peer network which is beyond the control of any central authority. What is this digital currency known as?

A. Bit Coins.

Q. Known as the Luhn algorithm it is used to check the authenticity of a debit or credit card. This technique was patented in 1960. Which personality is credited with this technique?

A. Peter Luhn (1876-1964) an IBM scientist.

Q. She is the only woman to have won the Nobel Prize for Economics so far. It was for the year 2009 for her work titled *'Economic governance, especially the Commons'*. Who is this special woman?

A. Elinor Ostrom.

Q. He impersonated as a international pilot, a Georgian doctor and a Louisiana parish prosecutor to commit cheque frauds worth millions of dollars. A movie by the name *'Catch me if you can'* has been made of him portraying his skills which were so unique that the FBI had to take his help in apprehending other cheque forgers. Identify this conman?

A. Frank Abagnale Jr.

Q. A well known British Prime Minister who was highly regarded said 'In finance everything that is agreeable is unsound and everything that is sound is disagreeable'. Can you identify the gentleman?

A. Winston Churchill.

Q. The term 'fiscal cliff' is engaging the US administration in a big way for formulation of their financial policies. Who used this term and where?

A. The US Federal Reserve Chairman Ben Bernanke used the term before the House Financial Services Committee.

Q. It has been decided by Greece that former finance minister George Papaconstantinou will face an enquiry into his handling of the 'Lagarde list' in 2010. What is this Lagarde list?

A. Christian Lagarde handed over the list of about 2,000 Greeks with money stashed in banks in Switzerland to Papaconstantinou when he was the finance minister of Greece in 2010 to investigate these potential tax evaders.

Q. In 1950s Life Insurance Corporation of India was made to invest about ₹ 1.24 crore in dubious companies owned by this person. LIC suffered because of this investment as it was a fraud. Who is this person well known to have committed this fraud?

A. Haridas Mundhra.

Q. He is known to be associated with diamond companies. Such individuals are known for their skills in cutting and polishing of diamonds. What is the name given to these professionals?

A. Diamantaires.

■■■

QUIZ TEN

Contemporary and Sundry Issues

Q. Narasimhan Committee Report had submitted its recommendations on the banking sector reforms in India during the 1990s. Who was M. Narasimhan?

A. M.Narasimhan was former Governor, Reserve Bank of India when the committee was instituted.

Q. This financial term was much in the news lately as economic analysts were debating the prospects of Greece leaving the Euro zone in the wake of its severe economic crisis. What is this word which expresses this apprehension?

A. Grexit.

Q. The monetary authority of the euro zone has the European Central Bank at the apex with the national central banks of the member countries assisting it. How is this authority expressed as?

A. Eurosystem.

Q. The European Central Bank with its enormous responsibility has its main headquarters located in one of the major member countries. Where is it located?

A. Frankfurt (Germany).

Q. A development bank is supporting the economic transition in the former East European countries and Soviet Republics for the last two decades. Which bank is being referred to?

A. European Bank for Reconstruction and Development (EBRD).

Q. Which two Indian public sector banks have been given the approval to open branches in Pakistan. Can you name them?

A. Punjab National Bank and Bank of India.

Q. In a mutual show of promoting enlargement of commercial ties between India and Pakistan, the Pakistani banks have also been granted permission to open branches in India. Which are these Pakistani banks?

A. National Bank of Pakistan and United Bank Ltd.

Q. World Bank had suspended providing aid to Myanmar in view of its continued domestic political issues. It recently resumed aid to it. After how many years did this resumption of aid to Myanmar start?

A. 25 years.

Q. The World Trade Organization which is an international body to promote trade among member countries by lessening of trade barriers did not have one major country as its member. Which is this country that we are talking about?

A. Russia.

Q. In a major development in relations between India and China, an Indian bank was given permission to open a branch in China. Which is this bank which became the first Indian bank to open a branch in China?

A. State Bank of India.

Q. RuPay is a new initiative in the Indian financial system. It has been promoted by National Payments Corporation of India as the domestic competitor to international players. What function is RuPay discharging?

A. it is a domestic card payment network.

Q. White label ATMs which were earlier not approved by the Reserve Bank of India have now been permitted. What is special about these white label ATMs?

A. These ATMs are managed by third party nonbanking companies.

Q. Implementation of GAAR has been postponed by the Indian government for the time being as it created unnecessary controversy. What is the meaning of GAAR?

A. The full form of GAAR is General Anti Avoidance Rules which attempts to prevent tax evasion.

Q. Reserve Bank of India has started a premier institution for the development of advanced financial research and learning. What is this institution known as?

A. Centre for Advanced Financial Research and Learning (CAFRAL).

Q. 'Superman', 'Hero', 'Captain Chaos' were among some names that the traders and brokers gave to each other in financial deals involving the Swiss banking giant UBS. These trades were discovered as part of investigations with regard to a huge scandal discovered in 2012. Which scandal is being referred to?

A. The manipulation of LIBOR by UBS Bank.

Q. Which top job in the international financial sector was recently advertised for the first time in 318 years?

A. The Governorship of the Bank of England.

Q. Reserve Bank of India has asked all banks to adopt the CTS 2010 standards latest by 31st July, 2013. What do we understand by CTS 2010?

A. Cheque Truncation System 2010.

Q. Number of international banks has faced stinging strictures from regulatory authorities in 2012. US Federal Reserve recently announced a record US 1.92 billion dollars settlement with HSBC Bank. This settlement is with regard to which transactions/events?

A. HSBC is accused of transferring billions of dollars for nations like Iran and enabled Mexican drug cartels to move money illegally through its American subsidiaries.

Q. Federation of Indian Chamber of Commerce and Industry (FICCI) has for the first time elected a woman as its President in 2012. Which lady has now occupied this post?

A. Naina Lal Kidwai.

Q. Why was the New York Stock Exchange NYSE shut down on 29th October, 2012, the first unscheduled closure after 2001?

A. Unprecedented natural catastrophe in the wake of Hurricane Sandy which hit New York and parts of USA.

Q. On this Diwali day in 2012, the Bombay Stock Exchange BSE had a special mahurut trading for start of a new year. Which event is being referred to?

A. The start of the Samvat calendar year 2069.

Q. According to reports the 2012s Nobel Prizes are not worth the usual money that it carries. It is being seen as a sign of the continuing euro zone crisis. What is the estimated worth of the 2012s Nobel Prizes?

A. Around 8 million kroners.

Q. What is the term used to describe the act of withdrawing currency and coins from circulation?

A. Demonetization.

Q. When a country gains from production of coins and currency after deducting expenses on production and distribution what is it known as?

A. Seigniorage.

Q. What is reserve money?

A. A foreign currency permanently held by a country's central bank and is used for international transactions.

Q. How would you describe 'Agio' in the context of handling of currency?

A. The fees charged by a bank for exchanging one form of currency or money into another that is more valuable.

Q. Gold is often described as fungible. What does it mean?

A. It means those goods or commodities which can be exchanged for something of the same kind, of equal value and quality.

Q. What is meant by mintage?

A. Usually refers to the quantity of coins that were produced at the mint for a given year

Q. Mint marks are supposed to identify the mints. What are these mint marks?

A. The marks on the coins indicating the mint which produced it.

Q. Jean Claude Trichet, Mervyn King and Ben Bernanke are huge names in the world of finance. Each of these individuals has occupied a similar post of authority in their respective countries. Which is that common post?

A. The post of the Governor of their respective central banks.

Q. These persons were born between 1946 and 1964 and were sources of many important cultural and economic changes. This group has been prime targets of the marketing professionals. How are they identified as?

A. Baby boomers.

Q. The successive generation of people born between 1977 and 1994 and considered as the children of baby boomers is also known by a particular name. What is that name?

A. Echo boomers.

Q. The Clearing Corporation of India Ltd., was set up in 2002 with a specific purpose. Can you mention it?

A. It is concerned with clearing and settlement in government securities.

Q. This international organization issues an annual Conception Perception Index since 1995. It is widely referred to while rating countries according to the perception in different parameters. Which is this organization?

A. Transparency International.

Q. This unit is used in calculating advertising rates of newspapers. It is a unit of newspaper space measurement and is usually 1 column wide by 1/14 inch deep. What is this unit known as?

A. Agate line.

Q. Multilevel marketing is a strategy adopted to increase the sales staff to push sales by having a system of graded commission payments. Which is the other commonly used term for it?

A. Pyramid marketing.

Q. Hall marking has become compulsory in the sale of gold jewellery. What does it mean?

A. Official certificate confirming the purity of gold sold as jewellery.

Q. It is a theory suggested by Richard Easterline in 1974 that beyond satisfaction of basic needs, increasing wealth of a country does not produce increasing happiness. What is the name given to this theory?

A. Easterline Paradox.

Q. Handwritten posters made in the 16th and 17th century England and considered as fore-runners of modern day advertising. What are they known as?

A. Siquis.

Q. Shown as a floater advertisement, it is a form of online advertisement which is a flash animation that runs though a webpage to capture the user's attention. By what term is it known as?

A. Shosh kele.

Q. There is a strategy which proposes that a multinational corporation should have a presence in Europe, USA and Asia preferably Japan. What is the name for this strategy?

A. Triad strategy.

Q. Corporations often resort to anticipatory pricing to ensure that their profit margins are protected. How does this work?

A. It means raising the prices by more than the anticipated cost increase in expectation of further inflation or price control measures by the government.

Q. It is a trans European automated RTGS express transfer system which balances out payment shortfalls and surpluses between central banks of the euro system as and when needed. By what name is this important mechanism known?

A. Target.

Q. In a historic move the international rating agency Standard & Poor down graded USA's sovereign rating from AAA to AA+. The fallout of this action was the ouster of the chief of Standard & Poor. Who was this personality?

A. Deven Sharma.

Q. In which instances would companies identify purchases made by consumers as arm chair buying?

A. Refers to purchase of selected goods using a catalogue while at home.

Q. Imported goods are at times kept with the Customs Department pending clearance and payment of customs duties. These goods are stored in a special place in control of the Customs department. What are these storage places known as?

A. Bonded warehouse.

Q. Which country was not supported by the IMF and World Bank with financial assistance during the Asian contagion crisis of 1997?

A. Vietnam.

Q. What term is used to describe a concentrated affirmative action of the government to push economic activity in the country?

A. Fiscal stimulus.

Q. Who is recognized as the founder of the World Economic Forum?

A. Klaus Schwab.

Q. Much of the Foreign Direct Investment in India comes from Mauritius than from any other major developed economies. Why does this happen?

A. There is a Double Taxation Avoidance Agreement with Mauritius.

Q. A company is required to get its financial instrument rated before offering it for investment to the public. If the company gets a 'AAA' rating what message does the investor receive?

A. The instrument is safe and recommended for investment.

Q. These exchanges trade in precious metals, metals, agricultural products, energy. They deal in future contracts and are basically speculative in nature as the price of any product is not fixed in an organized way. Which kind of exchanges are we talking about?

A. Commodity exchanges.

Q. This number contains critical information and appears on the reverse of a credit card. It is meant to be kept strictly confidential as unauthorized access to it can result in misuse of the card. Which is this number that we are referring to?

A. Credit verification value CVV number.

Q. Individuals are judged by their credit score given by credit information companies when requests for loans and credit facilities are examined by banks. Which credit score band is generally considered as worthy of getting credit from banks?

A. 800 to 900 is treated as a good credit score.

Q. When a banker talks about CDR in the context of a nonperforming asset, what is he talking about?

A. Corporate Debt Restructuring for enabling the nonperforming account to set right its financial problems.

Q. What term is used to define an economic situation when there is high rate of inflation with a simultaneous high rate of unemployment?

A. Stagflation.

Q. When was the first ATM opened for business in the world?

A. September 1969.

Q. What defines the faster way of buying/selling the same number of shares that earlier was sold/bought on the same day, in the same exchange at the market value?

A. Square-off.

Q. 'CAMELS' model is used by the Reserve Bank of India as part of their supervision and monitoring of commercial banks. This model is likely to be replaced shortly by yet another methodology. What purpose is CAMELS meant to serve?

A. It is the annual exercise carried out by RBI to assess the banks and rate them in the respective areas of their working.

Q. 'Creative destruction' is a word coined by an economist Joseph Schumpeter during his work on the evolutionary theory of economics. What did he try to convey?

A. It describes the growth of radically innovative companies in a space where the traditionally established companies are declining.

Q. Computerization in banks in India was introduced in the 1980s in a gradual way. The first visible signs of computerization were the installation of certain machines for replacing the ledger books for maintenance of deposit accounts. Which were these machines?

A. Advanced Ledger Posting Machines (ALPM).

Q. It is an association entrusted with the task of developing the mutual funds industry in India. It protects the interests of the mutual funds and the investors. Which is this body?

A. Association of Mutual Funds in India (AMFI).

Q. It is the world's premier maritime market for ship chartering, sale and purchase. A self-regulated London exchange which serves worldwide interests. Which is this exchange?

A. Baltic Exchange.

Q. 'Buddenbrooks' is a novel written by the German Nobel Prize winner Thomas Mann in 1901 which relates to family forms and their economic history. Linked to it is the term 'Buddenbrooks syndrome' which is used to relate to the nature of family businesses. How would you describe this term?

A. It refers to family businesses run by third generations which tend to run out of steam and lose their dynamism.

Q. INFINET is used by a large number of banks for funds and nonfunds based transfer messages. It has been developed by the Institute for Development and Research in Banking Technology. What is this INFINET?

A. Indian Financial Network.

Q. He is responsible for establishing and maintaining a sound and efficient accounting and financial reporting system in India. Which is this authority?

A. Comptroller General of Accounts.

Q. The Asian Development Bank was established in 1966 on the basis of recommendations of which authority?

A. Economic Commission for Asia and Far East (ECAFE).

Q. India is regarded as one of the most advanced markets when it comes to settlement of trade. There is a term known as 'rolling settlement' which is used in this context. What is meant by this term?

A. In a rolling settlement each trading day is considered as a trading period and trades executed during the day are settled based on net obligations for the day. Trades in rolling settlement are settled on T+2 basis, *i.e.,* on the second working day after a trade.

Q. Most ATMs are owned by banks. There are also those that are owned and operated by nonbanking companies. These ATMs are identified by a special name. What is that word?

A. White label ATMs.

Q. The departure of the chief executive of Barclays Bank has created quite a stir in banking circles in UK. He was considered very powerful but ultimately had to go as Barclays had been found in violation of various rules. Who is this high profile banker?

A. Robert Diamond.

Q. There is another instance of Jamie Dimon who presided over reckless risk taking to the extent of US$ 6 million, yet he remains the chief of this well known bank in the US. Which is this bank?

A. JP Morgan Chase.

Q. Reserve Bank of India decides on the entry of foreign banks in India. According to the WTO regulations, the RBI is bound to approve licensing for a certain number of branches of foreign banks annually, though more number of branches have been approved. What is the specified number?

A. 12 annually.

Q. The term 'Act of God' is widely used in insurance policies as these disasters are not usually covered. Which disasters are covered under an Act of God policy?

A. Such policies cover damages caused by natural disasters such as flood and hurricanes. Only specific natural disasters defined in the policy are covered. An Act of God policy does not cover earthquakes, which are covered separately.

Q. It is a type of negotiable financial security that is traded on the stock exchanges. It allows investors to hold shares in equity of other countries. What form of investment does it represent?

A. Depository receipts.

Q. It is felt that the GDP does not measure important considerations like inequality or environmental degradation while being an indicator of economic growth. There is therefore now emphasis on having a new indicator known as GDP+. What would this GDP+ measure?

A. Apart from mere income generation, it will capture other material conditions such as jobs, earnings, housing, quality of life, education, etc.

Q. Monthly income plans are compared to fixed deposits as different types of investments. What are the critical features of a monthly income plan?

A. These are hybrid instruments that invest a small part of their portfolio in equities and the remaining in debt instruments. It provides for payment of dividends at specified periodicities.

Q. Basel-III rules propose to bring in more clarity in the current rules by clearly defining different kinds of capital. What is the percentage banks are required to maintain in common equity as per Basel-III?

A. It should be 5.5 per cent as against 3.6 per cent currently.

Q. The phenomenon being discussed illustrates a movement in a variable, which falls initially but rises up to higher levels than before in the shape of an alphabet. When discussed in the context of a country's external account, it reveals that whenever there is depreciation in the currency's value, the trade deficit initially worsens but over time the exports rise. What is the name given to this phenomenon?

A. The J curve.

Q. By making certain provisions of the Banking Regulation Act applicable to a certain category of scheduled banks in 1966 they were brought under the regulatory purview of the Reserve Bank of India. Which was this class of scheduled banks?

A. Urban Cooperative Banks.

Q. These trade terms are published by the International Chamber of Commerce to make international trade easier by helping traders in different countries understand one another. What are these terms known as?

A. Incoterms.

Q. This employee sees himself as extremely loyal and diligent for his company. He attends to his work even when there is a strike in the company. By what name are such workers identified as?

A. Scab.

Q. Recently as part of unethical practices being adopted by influential personalities there was a frequent reference to their involvement in shell companies. What are these shell companies?

A. It is a company listed on the stock exchange but which does not trade.

Q. The word 'chop shop' was used for IT companies in India in the context of outsourcing of jobs by the US. What does this term convey?

A. It usually means those businesses whose products, services or equipment are of questionable quality.

Q. An organization has a system in which each employee reports to both a functional or divisional manager and a group project manager. What organizational structure would it be called?

A. Matrix structure.

Q. In the balance sheet of a nonprofit organization what term means the equivalent of owner's equity?

A. Net assets.

Q. The foreign exchange market of this country is referred to as the 'Rembrandt Market'. Which is this country?

A. Netherlands.

Q. Certain patent holders indulge in speculative law suits even though they have no intention to manufacture anything. How are they known?

A. As patent trolls.

Q. Name the country which is the latest to become a member of the International Monetary Fund. It is the 188th member of the Fund.

A. South Sudan.

Q. The Aadhar project is totally reliant on biometrics to achieve its objective of issuing the unique number to the majority of Indians. What are the different biometrics that are being used?

A. Finger prints and iris.

Q. China's growing affluence and influence over the world economy has made bonds issued by China very popular. A particular bond denominated in yuan is being issued in Hong Kong by Chinese government and companies. Which are these bonds?

A. Dim sum bonds.

Q. Balanced funds are a mix of equity and debt scrips with typically an investment ratio of 50:50. However, the Union Budget of 2006 approved SEBI's formula of the investment ratio which balanced funds are meant to follow. What was this ratio?

A. At least 65 per cent of equity exposure.

Q. In the 1990s the need was felt to put an end to monetization of fiscal deficit by printing more money. This led to significant increases in market borrowings of the government. What method was adopted by the government to address this issue of raising funds?

A. Auction of government securities.

Q. The NSE recently suspended trading for 15 minutes because of punching errors made by a dealer. At this time the lower circuit breaker kicked in. What is a circuit breaker?

A. It is a price limit set by the regulator on stock indices beyond which it cannot fluctuate in a day.

Q. SEBI had to institute guidelines for a new financing route in 2006 to prevent listed companies in India from relying too much on foreign capital. Known as qualified institutional placement (QIP). What does this provide for?

A. It helps a listed company to raise capital in the domestic market by means of issue of equity shares, fully and partly convertible debentures to a buyer of its choice.

Q. Qualified institutional placements can be issued only to a certain class of investors. Which are these investors?

A. Can be issued only to qualified institutional buyers (QIBs) who cannot be promoters or related to promoters of the issuing company.

Q. In 2012 India received its first investment through the qualified foreign investment route. What is special about qualified foreign investors (QFIs)?

A. They are individuals or trusts resident in a country that is a member of the FATF. Residents of a country signatory to the IOSCO or one that has signed a bilateral agreement with SEBI are also considered as QFI.

Q. In which investment segments of the market are QFIs eligible to invest?

A. In all three segments of the capital market, *i.e.,* mutual funds, equities and corporate debt.

Q. This pricing mechanism is named after the suicide pilots of World War II. It is the practice of selling loans at extremely low rates to capture the corporate market. By what name is this price mechanism known?

A. Kamikaze pricing.

Q. The Keogh plan is a financial scheme meant for self-employed people in the US. What is the purpose of this scheme?

A. It is meant to create a pension plan for the self-employed.

Q. This insurance plan is targeted at the small and medium enterprises sector meant primarily for the owner/chief executive of the firm. He is considered the most important person for the growth and success of the firm. What is the name given to such insurance plans?

A. Key person insurance.

Q. These fees are charged from car manufacturers for permitting its sale in the Indian markets. The fees are for checking if the cars comply with the Indian laws and regulations on safety standards. What is the term used to describe these charges?

A. Homologation fees.

Q. President Ronald Reagan of the US and Prime Minister Margaret Thatcher of UK in the 1980s are regarded to have promoted this brand of economic policy. They believed that the market should be left on its own, without government intervention, in making its decisions. It was a form of capitalism which trusted wealth to trickle down and identified individuals with the wealth and products they owned. What was the name given to this policy?

A. Gucci capitalism.

Q. Fair Isaac Corporation of the US has developed the credit score based on the credit history of borrowers. It is recognized as the global standard for assessing credit risk in the banking, mortgage and other financial lending markets. What is the name of this credit score?

A. FICO score.

Q. If a sequence of numbers which are 0,1,1,2,3,5,8,13,21,34,55,89… are mentioned and it is stated that each number in this sequence is the sum of the preceding two numbers, what information do you gather to identify the name given to this sequence?

A. Fibonacci numbers.

Q. If inclusive economies are attributable to forms of democratic governments then extractive economies would be identified with what form of government?

A. Autocratic rule.

Q. Dalal Street, Mint Street in Mumbai are frequently referred names in the financial world. With what would you identify Dalal Street?

A. It is the place where the Bombay Stock Exchange is located.

Q. Zombie banks are considered to have been in existence in Japan in 1990 when the country suffered a collapse in real estate and stock markets. What do these Zombie banks mean to you?

A. Refers to banking companies that are insolvent but continue to operate till its fate is resolved by closure or merger.

Q. Russia has decided to join this international organization after a long wait. Which is this organization?

A. World Trade Organization.

Q. It is an annual international event which is held in the month of January at Davos, Switzerland. The event has become a mega event for big corporations across the world. Which is this event?

A. The World Economic Forum meet.

Q. His name is Jim Yong Kim and is an American. Even though he is an anthropologist and physician he heads an important international financial body. Which is this organization?

A. World Bank.

Q. The acronym for this chamber of commerce is DICCI and is meant to represent the interests of business belonging to a particular section of the Indian community. Which is this organization?

A. Dalit Indian Chamber of Commerce and Industry.

Q. This facility is extended by the Reserve Bank of India to banks for management of their liquidity position on an overnight basis. What is this facility called?

A. Liquidity Adjustment Facility LAF.

Q. Infrastructure projects generally stretch for 15 years and more. Commercial banks are not considered as the appropriate financing institutions for infrastructure projects. Why is it so?

A. In infrastructure lending commercial banks have to depend on short-term funds for financing long-term projects. This can have adverse impact on their asset liability management.

Q. The pricing of loan products of commercial banks are now linked to a particular benchmark rate. Which is this rate?

A. Base rate of lending.

Q. What is the term used to describe an inflationary situation when monthly inflation exceeds 50 per cent or the three year cumulative inflation is in excess of 100 per cent?

A. Hyper inflation.

Q. Technology has revolutionized the way banking is being done in India since the last one decade. Banking services are now offered as 'any time any where banking'. Which particular technology mode has made this change possible?

A. Core banking solutions.

Q. Certain nonbanking finance companies which are registered with RBI are permitted to offer term deposit schemes to the public. What is the essential difference of these schemes as compared to the schemes of the commercial banks?

A. Deposits of nonbanking finance companies are not insured.

Q. These are negotiable receipts issued against goods received for storage. These receipts are acceptable as security for loans as they are considered as title to goods. Which type of receipts are we referring to?

A. Warehouse receipts.

Q. This watch was in the news recently for raising US $ 10.3 million in May 2012 which was nearly three times higher than the previous record in a crowd funded public offering. The watch is unique for displaying messages from the wearer's i phone and has a special name. What is that name which became famous?

A. PEBBLES.

Q. Largely due to the fallout from the collapse of the Lehman Bros, large banks in the US are preparing contingency plans in the event of their liquidation. The name given to these plans is similar to the terminology used for plans in case of deceased individuals. What is the term?

A. Living wills.

Q. This term describes the mindless consumption or passion for more. This expression of unbridled consumption is the trigger for the spread of consumerism in the society. Name this word which is music to the ears of the retailers?

A. Pleonexia.

Q. This legal process validates the authenticity of this document. It means the contents of the document are duly registered with the court of law. This document helps the bank in determining the legal heirs of a deceased accountholder for payment of the funds in the account. Identify this cerified document?

A. Probate.

Q. These trades are mostly for speculative purposes and for the institution's own profits which is totally unrelated to client business. Such trades undertaken by banks, brokerage firms have come for adverse comments from the regulators as it is leading to unethical practices. Which trade are we referring to?

A. Proprietary trade.

Q. It represents an index of measurement of the wealth of the manufacturing sector. The index is based on five crucial components for the manufacturing sector like new orders, inventory levels, production, supplier deliveries and employment opportunities. Which is this index?

A. Purchasing manager's index (PMI).

Q. It is the belief held by some that all problems can be resolved through negotiations without bothering to find out whether negotiations are the best way to reach the most appropriate solution. What term would you use to describe such a mindset?

A. Negomania.

Q. This is a situation being discussed in the context of banks charging a nominal interest rate for accepting deposits from public. It is a departure from the practice of offering interest on deposits. This situation is visible in Europe, as per Western media, in instances of banks in Europe charging interest on deposits in Danish krone and Swiss francs. Investors are reportedly shifting from keeping deposits in euro because of the perceived threat to the euro currency. The other situation is the possibility of banks having to pay interest to the Federal Reserve on their excess reserves. What is this unusual practice hinting at?

A. The concept of negative interest.

Q. Banks and financial institutions in India are required to maintain a certain amount of liquid assets like cash, gold and other short-term securities as reserves at all times. Which of the following explains this practice?

(*i*) CRR

(*ii*) SLR

(*iii*) PLR

(*iv*) Sub PLR

A. (*ii*)

Q. As part of its responsibilities SEBI has the power to take punitive action against companies for any wrong doing. In respect of which of the following issues can SEBI penalize a company?

(*i*) Violation of the provisions of the Banking Regulation Act

(*ii*) Violation of foreign portfolio investment guidelines

(*iii*) Noncompliance with provisions of the Negotiable Instruments Act

(*iv*) Infringement of the SARFAESI Act

A. (*ii*)

Q. 'Marketing myopia' is a term coined by Prof. Theodore Levitt to convey which of the following:

(*i*) a shortsightedness about business

(*ii*) a disjointed perception about the concept of marketing

(*iii*) overlooking the customer's preferences in the process of production

(*iv*) all of the above

A. (*iv*)

Q. In the context of the Indian economy which of the following was the earliest event to take place?

(*i*) nationalization of State Bank of India

(*ii*) the establishment of the Life Insurance Corporation of India

(*iii*) the introduction of the First Five-Year Plan

(*iv*) the enactment of the Banking Regulation Act

A. (*iv*)

Q. Which among the following associations is known as the forum of Pacific Rim Trade group of 21 countries which seeks to promote free trade and economic cooperation throughout the Asia-Pacific region?

(*i*) Mercosur

(*ii*) ASEAN

(*iii*) APEC

(*iv*) OPEC

A. (*iii*)

Q. Which of the following would best explain the automatic route to FDI which enables a foreign investor to bring in his capital?

(*i*) by prior permission of RBI

(*ii*) without the approval of FIPB

(*iii*) informing the RBI within one month of bringing in the funds without the need for approval of FIPB

(*iv*) informing the RBI and FIPB within two months of bringing in the investment

A. (*iii*)

Q. Reserve Bank of India has permitted the setting up of credit information companies in India. Which of the following is the first credit information company to have been established in India?

(*i*) CARE

(*ii*) CRISIL

(*iii*) CIBIL

(*iv*) Experian

A. (*iii*)

Q. In terms of Reserve Bank of India rules it has become compulsory for banks to implement which of the following?

(*i*) having photograph of the accountholder pasted on the passbook

(*ii*) mentioning the MICR code and IFSC code on the passbook of the depositors

(*iii*) indicating the details of the Customer Grievance Redressal Officer of the bank on the passbook of the depositor

(*iv*) all of the above

A. (*ii*)

Q. According to the new norms announced by RBI what is the minimum net worth required by a nonbanking finance company to set-up white label ATMs?

(*i*) ₹ 50 cr

(*ii*) ₹ 100 cr

(*iii*) ₹ 250 cr

(*iv*) ₹ 300 cr

A. (*ii*)

Q. Banks recently were offering a low rate of interest for some period on an adjustable rate mortgage to tempt borrowers and subsequently raise it to market rates. How are these type of double interest mortgage loans known as?

(*i*) below market rate

(*ii*) teaser rate

(*iii*) base rate

(*iv*) bridge loan rates

A. (*ii*)

Q. Paper currency does not have much life and needs to be withdrawn from circulation regularly. In what way is the Reserve Bank of India trying to resolve this issue?

(*i*) by printing currency on highly mechanized machines

(*ii*) by increasing the production of coins

(*iii*) by having polymer notes on trial basis

(*iv*) by proposing action against misuse of notes

A. (*iii*)

Q. A common form of lending for working capital to companies is through cash credit facility against hypothecation of stocks. Which of the following aptly describes this facility?

(*i*) it is a revolving credit facility against the security of stocks

(*ii*) it is a borrowing arrangement for purchase of goods

(*iii*) it is a credit facility where stocks in possession of the borrower legally belongs to the lender

(*iv*) borrowing facility against goods which are stored in godowns which are in control of the lender

A. (*iii*)

Q. To stop the fraudulent activity of multiple lending against mortgage of the same property, the Government of India has set-up a special agency. This agency would have records of mortgages created in the country and lending institutions have the facility of verifying the same. Which is this body?

(*i*) Central Electronic Registry

(*ii*) Registrar of Companies

(*iii*) Company Law Board

(*iv*) The Office of the Notary Public

A. (*i*)

Q. Branches of commercial banks are likely to face shortage of currency when payments are more in number. In such situations how do bank branches replenish their stock of currency?

(*i*) by approaching currency chests

(*ii*) by seeking assistance from the nodal branch of that bank at that location

(*iii*) by getting support from the main branch of SBI at that location

(*iv*) all of the above

A. (*iv*)

Q. Which of the following would differentiate appropriately the difference between a post office savings account and a bank savings account?

(*i*) there is no cheque facility with post office savings account (*ii*) interest on savings account in banks are paid as per individual bank rules, while interest on post office savings accounts are determined by the government

(*iii*) passbooks are not issued by post offices for their savings accounts

(*iv*) post offices do not participate in the clearing process

A. (*ii*)

Q. National Payments Corporation of India is a Reserve Bank of India appointed body to oversee the working of the financial sector. Which area does it supervise?

(*i*) payments through the clearing house

(*ii*) payments and settlements system in the country

(*iii*) payments through the electronic mode

(*iv*) payments through RTGS and NEFT

A. (*ii*)

Q. RBI had appointed the Malegam committee to recommend changes in the working of an important area of the financial sector. Many of the recommendations have been accepted. Which is this area?

(*i*) the capital markets

(*ii*) mutual funds industry

(*iii*) microfinance sector

(*iv*) customer service in banks

A. (*iii*)

Q. Which of the following is the apex institution which handles refinance for agriculture and rural development in India?

(*i*) RBI

(*ii*) NABARD

(*iii*) SIDBI

(*iv*) IFCI

A. (*ii*)

Q. India Infrastructure Financial Corporation Ltd., has been observed to buy long-term loans of substantial amounts from banks mid-way through the tenure of the loan. This type of buying and selling of loans in the banking sector is popularly known as:

(*i*) infrastructure financing

(*ii*) take out financing

(*iii*) consortium financing

(*iv*) syndicated lending

A. (*ii*)

Q. Many companies approach the foreign markets to raise funds. What is this process/ instrument known as?

(*i*) participatory notes

(*ii*) foreign currency non-resident accounts

(*iii*) foreign currency convertible bonds

(*iv*) foreign direct investment

A. (*iii*)

Q. Customers are required to know the IFSC code of the bank branch where they have their account. In what way does it help?

(*i*) it is necessary for using the debit card

(*ii*) it is essential in electronic transfer payments

(*iii*) the code has to be mentioned while making complaints to the Ombudsman

(*iv*) required for mobile banking

A. (*ii*)

Q. Where in India was the first model e court launched in 2009 by the Chief Justice of India?

(*i*) Ahmedabad

(*ii*) Mumbai

(*iii*) Chennai

(*iv*) Bengaluru

A. (*i*)

Q. Which of the following economists can be credited for using the term 'globalization' first?

(*i*) Theodore Levitt

(*ii*) Alan Greenspan

(*iii*) Paul Krugman

(*iv*) Henry Paulson

A. (*i*)

Q. Which of the following institutions has become synonymous with the growth of micro-financing in the world?

(*i*) Doha Bank

(*ii*) Grameen Bank

(*iii*) Habib Bank

(*iv*) Sewa Bank

A. (*ii*)

Q. In economic theory the concept of social welfare and economic welfare are explained in a way that the two could be termed as one of the following options.

(*i*) two independent factors

(*ii*) partially related to each other

(*iii*) synonymous with each other

(*iv*) one as subset of the other

A. (*iv*)

Q. Which of the following options best describes the current account balance while calculating 'balance of payments' for a country?

(*i*) exports less imports

(*ii*) imports only

(*iii*) trade balance plus capital account balance

(*iv*) cost of domestic production plus production for exports

A. (*iii*)

Q. The term PIIGS was being regularly used while discussing the continuing financial crisis in Europe. To which of the following group is the term related?

(*i*) Portugal Italy Ireland Greece Spain

(*ii*) Panama Iceland Ireland Greece Spain

(*iii*) Panama Italy Iceland Greece Spain

(*iv*) Portugal Italy Iceland Greece Sweden

A. (*i*)

Q. There are reportedly 30 diamond mines operating in the world as of now. In which of the following countries are the most important mines discovered?

(*i*) Southern Africa, Western Canada

(*ii*) Siberia

(*iii*) Only (*i*)

(*iv*) Both (*i*) and (*ii*)

A. (*iv*)

Q. Which of the following cities first started diamond mining?

(*i*) Venice

(*ii*) London

(*iii*) Istanbul

(*iv*) None of the above

A. (*iv*)

Q. What particular substance is diamond composed of?

(*i*) Silica

(*ii*) Glass

(*iii*) Carbon

(*iv*) All of the above

A. (*iii*)

Q. With which of the following you would not associate the Reserve Bank of India?

(*i*) issuance of currency notes

(*ii*) maintaining price stability and ensuring adequate flow of credit to the productive sectors

(*iii*) to facilitate external trade and developing a foreign exchange market in India

(*iv*) formulating and monitoring the monetary and credit policy

A. (*ii*)

Q. The recommendations of the Basel committee relate to which aspect of banking operations?

(*i*) Priority sector lending

(*ii*) Risk management

(*iii*) Microfinancing

(*iv*) Retail banking

A. (*ii*)

Q. The term M3 is frequently used in financial literature. Which of the following would best describe M3?

(*i*) currency in circulation on a particular day

(*ii*) total value of foreign exchange on a particular day

(*iii*) the total revenues collected in a year through taxes

(*iv*) none of the above

A. (*iv*)

Q. Foreign direct investment and foreign institutional investment are both linked to investments in a country. Which of the following statements appropriately represents an important difference between the two concepts?

(*i*) FDI brings in capital, while FII helps better management skills and technology

(*ii*) FDI targets specific sectors, whereas FII helps in increasing capital availability

(*iii*) FDI flows only into the secondary market, while FII enters the primary market

(*iv*) FII is regarded as more stable than FDI

A. (*ii*)

Q. If the International Monetary Fund is being discussed which of the following statements would be the most appropriate for it?

(*i*) it can grant loans to any country

(*ii*) it can provide financial aid only to developed countries

(*iii*) it is meant to provide loans only to member nations

(*iv*) it can grant loans to the central bank of a country

A. (*iii*)

Q. The revenues collected by the Government of India through taxes and other receipts for the conduct of government business are credited to which of the following accounts?

(*i*) Contingency Fund of India

(*ii*) Consolidated Fund of India

(*iii*) Public Debt Fund

(*iv*) Central Revolving Fund

A. (*ii*)

Q. The financial sector reforms which were initiated in the 1990s covered which of the following issues?

(*i*) deregulation of interest rates

(*ii*) entry of private companies in the insurance sector

(*iii*) lowering of the cash reserve ratio and statutory liquidity ratio

(*iv*) all of the above

A. (*iv*)

Q. The Lion capital which appears on the face of Indian currency notes was taken from which of the following locations?

(*i*) Sanchi

(*ii*) Bodh Gaya

(*iii*) Sarnath

(*iv*) Hampi

A. (*iii*)

Q. Payment of income tax in India is being regularly simplified. Which is the latest mode for payment of income tax?

(*i*) Internet

(*ii*) ATM

(*iii*) RTGS

(*iv*) NEFT

A. (*ii*)

Q. 'Operation Twist' is the term used to describe the strategy of the US Federal Reserve related to a particular issue. Which of the following is it?

(*i*) increasing outsourcing activities

(*ii*) reducing interest rates to promote long-term loans

(*iii*) curtailing assistance to various nations

(*iv*) selling gold reserves in the market

A. (*ii*)

Q. Banks get the benefit of using huge funds when cheques are sent in clearing as there is usually two to three days gap between debit of the accountholder's account and credit to the account of the payee of the cheque. There is a special term to define this phenomenon. What is this word?

(*i*) float money

(*ii*) suspense money

(*iii*) unaccounted funds

(*iv*) all of the above

A. (*i*)

Q. In which of the following banks has the government purchased the entire stake of the Reserve Bank of India?

(*i*) State Bank of India

(*ii*) Central Bank of India

(*iii*) Corporation Bank

(*iv*) UCO Bank

A. (*i*)

Q. Which of the following would you identify as a depository in India handling dematerialized shares?

(*i*) Multi Commodity Exchange

(*ii*) National Stock Exchange

(*iii*) Central Depository Services Ltd.

(*iv*) Forward Markets Commission

A. (*iii*)

Q. The World Economic Outlook is a prestigious publication which is issued regularly. Which of the following organizations publishes it?

(*i*) The International Monetary Fund

(*ii*) World Bank

(*iii*) OECD

(*iv*) World Trade Organization

A. (*i*)

Q. SIDBI is an apex financial institution for the small and medium scale enterprises in India. It was created as a result of which of the following actions?

(*i*) one of the departments of RBI was converted to an independent set-up

(*ii*) a part of the activities of NABARD was separated

(*iii*) created out of IDBI Ltd., for greater focus on the small and medium scale enterprises

(*iv*) set-up by the federations of the small and medium sector industries

A. (*iii*)

References

Ferguson, Niall, (2009). *The Ascent of Money: A Financial History of the World*. London: Penguin.

Levitt, Stephen, D. and Stephen, J. Dubner, (2005/06). *Freakonomics: A Rogue Economist Explores the Hidden Side of Everything*. New York: Harpertorch.

Lewis, Michael, (2011). *Boomerang: Travels in the New Third World*. New York: Norton and Co.

Tannan, M.L., (1977). *Banking Law and Practice in India*. Bombay: Thacker & Co. Ltd.

Varshney, P.N., (2011). *Banking Law and Practice*. New Delhi: Sultan Chand & Sons.

Newspapers and Magazines

Business India

Business Line

Business Standard

Business Today

Business World

Caravan

ET Wealth

Economic Times

Financial Express

Mint

Outlook Business

Outlook Money

Websites

Bloomberg News

Business Line E-paper

Business Standard E-paper

CNBC News

Financial Express E-paper

Financial Times

Financial Times lexicon

Indian Banks' Association

Indian Institute of Banking and Finance

Insurance Regulatory Development Authority

Investopedia.com

Livemint.com

Reserve Bank of India

Securities and Exchange Board of India

Journals

IIBF *Vision*

Quest

■■■